Myths and Legends

THE GOLDEN HOARD

six prints by Bee Willey

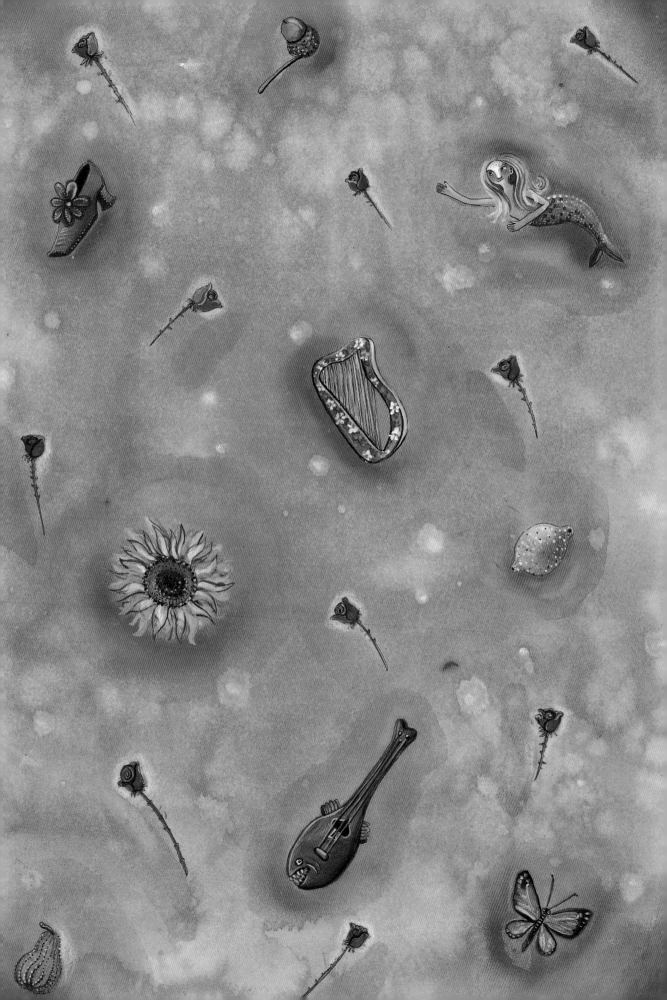

# The
# GOLDEN
# HOARD

# Geraldine McCaughrean

## MYTHS and LEGENDS of the WORLD

### THE GOLDEN HOARD

*Illustrated by*
**Bee Willey**

Orion
Children's Books

*For Ailsa*

*If I could I would give you all the stories in the world*

First published in Great Britain in 1995
by Orion Children's Books
a division of the Orion Publishing Group Ltd
Orion House
5 Upper St Martin's Lane
London WC2H 9EA

Text copyright © Geraldine McCaughrean 1995
Illustrations copyright © Bee Willey 1995
Designed by Dalia Hartman

The right of Geraldine McCaughrean and Bee Willey to be identified as the author
and illustrator of this work has been asserted.

A catalogue record for this book is available from the British Library

Printed in Italy

ISBN 1 85881 201 1

# Contents

# The Golden Wish

A GREEK MYTH

THERE WAS once a fool. Of course there have been far more fools than one, and fools more often than once. But this particular fool was a king, so his foolishness mattered. He lived in Greece, at the foot of Mount Olympus, and his name was Midas. All he thought about was gold. All day, while the golden sun shone, he shut himself away in dark vaults counting tinny gold. All night long, while the golden firelight glimmered, he shivered over his accounting books reading the words to himself:

*Twelve bars of gold in my vaults*
*Twenty plates of gold on my table*
*Ten rings of gold on my wife*
*Four hundred gold coins in my tax coffers . . .*

1

The centaurs, unlike Midas, valued only fun and wine. One day (and on many others, too) a centaur took too many drinks and stumbled into Midas's garden.

"I am lost," he told the King.

Midas set the centaur on the right road for Olympus.

"Such a friend! Such kindness!" exclaimed the centaur, joyfully kicking up his heels. "How can I thank you? A wish? I shall grant you one wish."

Now Midas knew that these centaurs, these horse-men, grazed on the slopes of Olympus and drew magic from the holy mountain. His heart leapt to his mouth. "A wish? You mean anything? I wish that everything I touch turns to gold!" He said it quickly, before the centaur could withdraw the offer.

"Ah. I should have warned you. People have asked that of the gods before, and . . ."

"Your magic isn't powerful enough! I knew it."

"Oh, I can grant it," said the centaur, flicking flies with his long tail. "But you'll be sorry."

"*No, I won't!*"

The centaur pronounced no spell. He did not spit or clap or chant. So when he trotted away towards Olympus, Midas felt sure no magic had passed between them. "Boaster! Braggart!" he yelled after the galloping horse-man, and pounded the garden wall with his fist.

The wall felt smooth under his hand. It gleamed and glittered in the sunlight.

Gold.

Midas ran to his treasury and touched all the brass coins. They instantly shone gold - and not just the coins, but the jars they were in and the door of the treasure-house.

Gold.

Midas ran through the palace stroking and slapping every stool, bench, table and urn. They all turned to gold. His china and statues, his weapons and chariot all shone, more exquisite and precious than anything he had ever dreamed of owning. "When we charge into battle," he told his horse, patting its fat rump, "we shall dazzle our enemies, you and I!"

The horse did not respond. It stood quite silent and quite still between the traces of the chariot: a perfect gold statue of a horse. Midas was a little startled, but after a moment he shrugged his shoulders. It made a fine statue for his new golden palace. And fresh horses can be bought by the dozen if a man has the gold to buy them.

"A feast! A festival! Where's my Chancellor? Where's my cook? Invite everyone! Spare no expense! Let the world know that Midas has gold! Midas has gold enough to buy up every sword, every horse, every acre of land in the world! I shall be unconquerable! I shall be worshipped! I shall be the envy of every man from the poorest beggar to the richest millionaire! I shall *be* the richest millionaire! A millionaire a million times over! Cook, where are you?"

His cook rushed in, carrying the King's lunch. He could not help but stare round him at all the changes to the room - the gold ornaments, the

golden furniture. Midas snatched the bread impatiently off the tray and bit it. "Huh? What are you feeding me these days? Rocks?" When he threw down the bread in disgust, it skidded across the golden floor. A golden loaf.

Food too, then? Midas took a drink to steady his nerves.

At least, he tried to take a drink. But the wine, as it touched his lip, turned to gold, to solid, metallic, unyielding gold. Midas stared. The cook stared. "Don't just stand there! Fetch me something I can eat!" And he gave the man a push.

Ah well, there are more cooks in the world, for a man with limitless gold.

Midas sat down on the ground beside the golden statue of his cook. His clothes, one by one, in touching his skin, had been turning to gold around him, and he found that he was suddenly very, very weary from wearing them.

He had not meant it to be like this when he asked the centaur to . . . He had not meant food and clothes and people and horses . . .

Midas began to wonder. How long does it take for a man to starve to death?

Just then, his queen came in and, ahead of her, their little daughter. Midas tried to warn her. He tried to stop the girl running to him with outstretched arms. But the child was too young to understand. Her little fingers closed round Midas's hand - and stiffened, and grew cold, and could not be prised open again. Her face and features, too, hardened and set, and the eyes were plain gold orbs in their golden sockets, the golden mouth frozen, for ever half-open to speak.

"Oh Zeus! Oh you gods! No! Not my daughter! Not my little girl!" He ran past the Queen, past the guards, his arms burdened with the monstrous weight of a small clinging golden child. He ran out of his golden palace and its golden gardens: the flowerheads jangled as he brushed by them. He ran across golden grass to a forest and blighted it with a golden canker. He ran through orchards till the sight of the fruit maddened him with hunger. He started up the rocky slopes of Olympus, staggering under the

weight of his lifeless daughter.

How long does it take for a man to die of loneliness? Or a broken heart?

"Take back this curse! What did I ever do to you that you punish me like this?" When he kicked off his heavy golden shoes, the golden grass spiked his soles like needles.

"Curse? I thought I granted you a wish," said a familiar voice. The centaur trotted out of a nearby cave.

"I was a fool! I see that now! I was a fool! But does a man deserve to lose his daughter - to die - just because he's a fool?"

The centaur picked a few stalks of grass and nibbled them thoughtfully. "I did try to warn you. Perhaps I've done you a favour, after all, if it has taught you something about yourself . . ."

"Wonderful! I shall die wise, then!" said Midas.

The centaur blew through his lips. "If you take my advice, you'll go to the river and jump in," he said.

"*Kill* myself, you mean?" gasped Midas.

"No, you fool. *Wash* yourself."

At the banks of the river Midas did not hesitate. If the water did not turn to gold and crush him, then the weight of the metal child clasping his hand might pull him under and drown him. But he did not care. He flung himself into the river, and its water closed over his head. As he surfaced, his daughter surfaced beside him, spluttering and terrified, not knowing why or how she came to be swimming. "Father? Where are all your clothes?"

Together they carried buckets of water back to the palace, and flung it over cook and horse, over stool and table and coins. The colour of gold was loathsome to Midas, and he was not content until he had undone all the alchemy of his magic golden touch.

Never again did he dream of gold - except in nightmares. Never again did he yearn to own gilded ornaments and mounds of yellow riches. No, no! For Midas had learned his lesson, hadn't he?

Now he thought about jewels, instead.

# Shooting the Sun

A CHINESE MYTH

IMAGINE A TREE with a spread of branches and twigs as intricate as the blood vessels of an eye. Imagine its trunk twelve thousand spans high, roots plunging as far as the earth's hot core. Imagine a rookery of nests in the topmost branches, each the size of a galleon, each the cradle of a boy-child. And imagine the parents of those children, Di Jun, god of the eastern sky, and his wife Xi He.

In the ancient days of China, Di Jun and Xi He had ten sons, strong and handsome, each with a yellow suit, a scarf of orange and a cloak of flame. Each morning their proud mother whistled up the dragon which lay coiled around the great tree where she lived, and harnessed it to her chariot. Then, with one of her boys beside her, she drove to the edge of the eastern sky. There she set him down - Lung or Wu, Yanxi, Ming or Xang - and

7

with a last comb of his hair or damp finger to clean a smut off his nose, she left him there to walk the path across the sky. Each boy, you see, was a sun.

Many footprints tamped flat that blue, celestial path. For many thousands of mornings this same routine took place. But after a thousand years more, the boy-suns grew into boisterous, roistering louts too vain and wilful to do as their parents told them.

They liked to do everything together, and had no patience to wait ten days for their turn to light the world. Thus it came about, in the reign of Emperor Yao, that the Chinese Empire was blighted by a terrible vandalism. The leaves of the trees blackened and curled. The feathers of the cranes singed and moulted. Fishponds boiled and the rhododendrons burned like a million campfires on the hills of China. For there were ten suns burning all at once in the sky.

Corners which were gardens in the morning were deserts by the evening. Even nightfall did not bring a respite from the dreadful heat, the fearful drought, for the ten suns stayed in the sky all the time, playing sports and horsing wildly about. The earth below never knew the healing balm of cool darkness. The people clamoured at the Emperor's gate, begging him to do something. And each one of them had ten shadows at his feet,

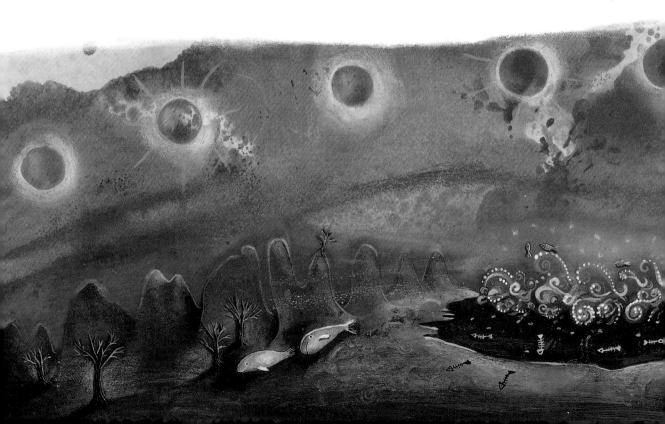

because of the ten glaring suns in the sky.

Emperor Yao travelled across the ocean to the valley where the great tree grew, and he stood at the bottom and hailed Di Jun with all the respect that one king can offer another. "O marvellous ruler of the eastern sky, will you not ask your royal children to do as they once did, and walk the sky's path one at a time? The world is burning, the sea is steaming, and soon the only water left will be the tears of my people!"

The great tree shook in every limb. "O Emperor, no words are harder for a father to speak, but my sons are my shame! They have lost all respect for the word of their parents. Neither their mother nor I can shame them into obedience. Not .threats or bribes, not shouts or politeness humble these roaring boys! But tell your people I will not abandon them to fire and scorching. I have sent Yi the great archer of the sky, with his red bow and ten white arrows, to shoot down my delinquent sons!" On an outer branch of the tree, Xi He could be seen sobbing, while her dragon lay panting far below her, half-buried in crisp leaves fallen from the drought-stricken tree.

Emperor Yao bowed low and returned to his people with the good news. Though no one saw Yi in person, nor the red curve of his bow, many claimed to have seen his white arrows streaking skywards.

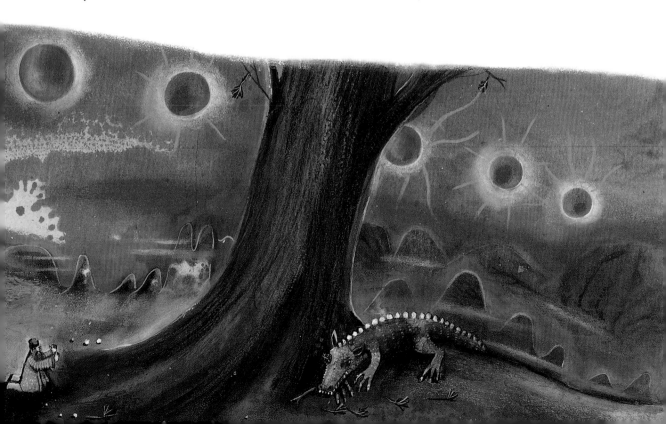

*BANG!* One sun exploded in a ball of fire and spun in the sky like a Catherine wheel. As it fell, it changed colour - from white-hot to blood-red, from red to umber, umber to brown. Then each flame turned to a black feather in the body of a black crow, and the dead crow landed, feet up, with an arrow in its breast.

*BANG! BANG!* The suns fell like oranges from a shaken tree. Four, five, six. "Blessings on you, Di Jun!" cried the people. "You have valued our lives and our world above the lives of your ten sons!"

"Ten?" said the Emperor to himself with a start. He shielded his eyes and glanced up at the sky. Four suns were left, blazing down on the earth, roasting the bears in their caves, the turtles in their shells. "Will he shoot down all ten?" Suddenly it dawned upon Yao that Di Jun meant every last son to die. Yi the archer had ten arrows in his quiver, and when he fired the last one, the world would be plunged into total darkness. Instead of too great a heat, there would be none, and the birds would shiver in the trees and the fish be frozen in ponds of solid ice.

"Quick!" he said to the courtier standing beside him. "Run to where Yi is shooting, and steal the last white arrow in his quiver!"

Without question, the courtier set off to run - over parched meadow and dry stream, over charred bushes and burned forests. As he ran, the shadows which streamed out behind him decreased in number from four to three, and a black crow fell at his feet. As he ran, the temperature dropped, and another black crow fell.

Just as the courtier glimpsed Yi, his red bow as bent as any dogwood tree, the bowstring twanged and a ninth sun exploded in a whirligig of flame. A ninth crow plummeted to the ground.

Yi reached behind him and felt for the last arrow. He fumbled, looked in his quiver, then looked around. He saw nothing but the dust flying up behind a running man who did not stop when called.

He did not stop, in fact, till he reached the court of Emperor Yao, and presented his emperor with a single white arrow. Meanwhile, the last of Di Jun's suns was running towards the eastern horizon, too afraid to look behind him. He disappeared over the rim of the world, and night fell on the Day of Di Jun's Anger.

That one son was so frightened by what had happened that he might never have shown his face again in heaven. "The Celestial Bowman will shoot me down, Mama!" he wailed piteously.

But his mother simply bundled him into her dragon chariot next morning, and ordered him out again at the edge of the eastern sky. "So he will, if you don't behave yourself better in future, my lad!" and she pointed an imperious finger out along the sky-blue pathway.

As soon as his back was turned, she watched him begin his journey with her head on one side and a fond smile on her face. She was so grateful to Emperor Yao for saving the life of her youngest son that she allowed him sometimes to ride in her dragon chariot, and they would tour the boundaries of China together discussing such things as tea and chess.

# George and the Dragon

### A PERSIAN MYTH

AS THE SUN rose, the town opened its gates, as if it were yawning. As if it were yawning, it shut them again. Left outside were a goose and a nanny goat - the last animals in the whole town. The goose honked balefully, the goat pressed itself against the gate, sensing danger. Then a large shadow swamped them in darkness, a flash of flame burned up the shadow, and goat and goose were gone. When the people of the town peeped over their high palisades, nothing remained but a scattering of charred bones and a sprinkling of white feathers. The dragon had been fed for one more day.

No one any longer left the town to tend their crops or travel to market. They simply waited, prisoners within their own walls, while the besieging dragon circled them, scratching its hide against the wood walls, sharpening its claws on the gates. It had slithered out of the lake - a beast longer than night and hungrier than quicksand. Its scales ran with slimy sweat, and its jaws dripped acid saliva. Wherever it trod, the grass withered and died. The stench wilted the cherry blossom and cankered apples on the bough.

Princess Sabra had seen the beast from the top window of her tall room, high in the royal palace, where she watched for help to come. But no help came, for no one knew of the town's plight, or if they did, they dared not come near. Having seen the dragon once, Sabra hung her cloak over the window so that she might never see it again. But she could not shut out the sound of crying in the streets, of screams and shouting, of fights and quarrelling. All the animals in the city had been fed to the dragon. Now the King had given orders for a lottery.

The name of every man, woman and child was entered in the lottery, and whosoever's name was drawn would be turned out to feed the dragon. The King closed his doors against the angry protesters. "It is necessary," was all he would say, shouting through the thickness of the door. "Do you want the dragon to tear down the city walls looking for its food?"

And the dragon found the taste of human flesh to its liking, and came earlier each morning to be fed.

Then, one day, the knocking at the palace door did not stop. "Open, Lord King! Princess Sabra's name has been drawn in the lottery!"

"No! No! Her name should never have been entered! My daughter? Never!" But his subjects (though they loved their princess dearly) had no pity left in their hearts. Terror had wrung them dry of it. "We have lost our loved ones - our husbands, our wives, our sons and daughters. Give up the Princess Sabra, for she must feed the dragon in the morning!"

A flagpost stood outside the gate. To this, each day, the victim was tied with strong rope, blessed with kisses and tears, and left alone to await the dragon's hunger. On the summer morning when Sabra took her place beneath the flag, the sky overhead was full of mare's-tail clouds, and the fields full of poppies. Birds sang in the scorched orchards, and the sun glinted on the poisoned lake. Above her, the blood-red banner flicked its lolling tongue, and the city bell began to toll dully - *chank chank chank.*

Suddenly, a horseman appeared on the skyline: she might not have seen him but for the sunlight gleaming on his metal helmet and the dazzling white of the shield across his back. He stopped to look around him, wondering, no doubt, at the blackness of the countryside, charred, burned, dead. Sabra wondered, in turn, whether to shout a warning. There was still time for him to escape, whereas everyone in her city was surely doomed, one by one, to die in the dragon's jaws.

All at once, the birds stopped singing. Through the soles of her feet, Sabra felt the ground tremble. Through the walls of her soul, she could feel fear crushing her heart. Out of the pool, out of its subterranean lair, the dragon raised its head to see what morsel waited by the city gate. Out it heaved itself, lidless eyes rolling, nostrils dilating. Its tongue unfurled suddenly from behind its teeth, forked and flickering. There was a smell of sulphur and filth.

Sabra opened her mouth to scream, but fear was strangling her. Instead, she heard a voice, loud and calm and demanding of attention. "So. I have found you at last," said the knight. "Evil made flesh."

The dragon cast a look over its shoulder, and the lobeless earholes sucked in the words. It looked the knight over and then turned back towards Sabra. No meal so delectable had yet been placed before it, and nothing could disrupt its lust to feed.

But as it scuttled towards her, on bowed legs and splayed feet, the knight rode at full tilt and crashed his horse, flank against flank, sidelong into the beast.

It turned in irritation and snapped, but the knight was too quick, and galloped out under its tail. "Know this, beast, that I am George of Lydda and the shape of your undoing. I am here to make an end of you!"

The baggy jaw gaped in a grimace like a laugh. A ball of fire burst at the horse's feet as the dragon spat its contempt. The mare reared up, her mane singed short by the heat, but George stayed in the saddle, spurring her forwards once more, driving his spear deep into the dragon's haunch.

The beast seemed to feel no more pain than from a bee-sting, and rubbed himself against the town wall, breaking off the shaft of the spear

and opening a gap in the long palisade. Its tail brushed Sabra as it turned, and the razor-sharp scales snagged her dress to ribbons. With a single blow of a webbed claw, it knocked over the knight's white mare.

George rolled clear, drawing from the side of his saddle a broadsword, as bright and as long as day. And there, where he had risen, he took his stand, white shield raised over his head. A torrent of fire splashed over the snowy heraldry and turned it to silver ash, but from beneath the burning buckler the knight struck out - a slash to the snout, a lunge to the breast, a charge into the green coils of snaking, dragony neck. Sabra shut her eyes. She could not remember how to breathe, how to make her heart beat. A carpet of fire unrolled at her feet and set her dress alight.

But a hand extinguished the flames, and another brushed her long hair back off her face. "The beast is down, lady. If I might borrow your sash, you may see foulness conquered by purity."

Sabra opened her eyes and saw George loop her sash around the dying dragon's throat. Its thrashing tail lay still, its laboured breathing ceased with a quiet sigh, and the fire of wickedness burning in its soul went out like a penny candle. "I fought you in the name of Christ Jesus, who is goodness made flesh," George whispered into the beast's ear. "So you see, you stood no chance."

Then the gates of the town opened like a great cheer, and out poured the people to stare, the children to clamber over the dragon's carcass. The King embraced George, and thanked him a thousand times. "Stay! Stay and marry the Princess Sabra and rule the kingdom after I am dead . . . !"

But George thanked him graciously, exchanged smiles with the Princess, then remounted his horse. "I am on a journey," he said, "which does not end here." Sabra watched her knight ride away, she noticed that his shield was no longer scorched, but white again, and that a red cross embellished it now; a simple blood-red cross.

# Skinning Out

AN ETHIOPIAN MYTH

WHY GO to all the trouble of creating people and then let them wear out? It is like building a cart and not nailing on the wheels: sooner or later they will fall off - and what good is the cart then?

The Maker, who moulded and shaped the Galla people, was neither forgetful nor slipshod. You may see it in the people - as tall and willowy as fishing rods and beautiful as ebony. And his intent never was to let their beauty wane. But of course the blazing sun over Ethiopia dries soft skin and puckers it into wrinkles. Though the babies gleam like stones from the bottom of a stream, the old men and women bend and wrinkle like the tree whose roots can no longer reach water.

"Go to the Galla, Holawaka," said The Maker to his messenger bird, "and tell them, when their skins start to wrinkle and to weigh heavy, to slip them off and leave them where they fall. Underneath hides a new beauty, as the butterfly hides within the caterpillar."

The brightly coloured bird, who sat preening her purple feathers with a beak of scarlet, cocked her head. "Very well," she said. "But how shall I know the Galla from the rhinoceros or the giraffe, from the hyena or the lioness? These creations of yours all look the same to me - no feathers, no beaks, no plumes . . ."

"The Galla are as tall and willowy as fishing rods and beautiful as ebony," said The Maker. "How you do *talk*, Holawaka."

So Holawaka flew down to the earth, still talking, but only to herself. Presently she met Tortoise. "This is not the Galla," she said, "for it is squat and round and its face is far from lovely." So she flew on by. Soon, however, she saw Snake.

"Now this fellow *is* as tall and willowy as a fishing rod and as beautiful as . . . what was it, again? Ah yes, beautiful as emeralds." And she asked, "Would you care to know the secret of staying young and never growing old?"

Snake, not surprisingly, cared a great deal. So Holawaka showed him

how to slough his skin and slither out. The skin was left behind, delicate as paper, diamond-patterned and translucent in the sunshine.

"Of course, if I had been The Maker," said Holawaka, who liked to talk, "I would have given you people feathers to fly with. Then you could have nested among the treetops and dived for fish in the lakes, and left single feathers like licks of paint on the ground." On and on Holawaka talked, though Snake had long since gone to tell his children the secret of staying young and never growing old, and she was speaking only to his sloughed skin. When she noticed this, she hopped back into the sky and home to The Maker's orchard where she perched on his fruit trees.

"Did you give the message to the Galla?"

"Yes, yes . . . though I'd have called him *long* rather than *tall*."

By the time the mistake was realized, the world was set in its ways, and The Maker was busy elsewhere. That is why the men and women of the Galla (and the rest of us for that matter) grow wrinkled and old with passing time, and the passage of many suns. Don't trouble to go looking for Snake to learn his secret. You will never find him - only empty snakeskins, crackling and translucent.

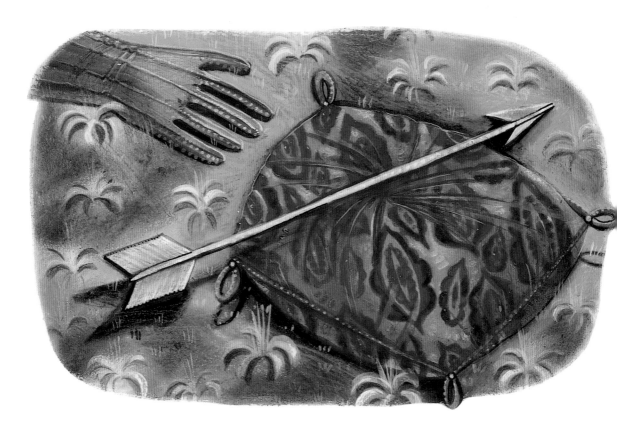

# Robin Hood and the Golden Arrow

AN ENGLISH LEGEND

ENGLAND WAS a country in despair. When the wind blew through its forests, the trees groaned and the leaves sighed. It was a country ruled by foreign invaders, and while the Normans fed richly off the fat of the land, the conquered Saxons made do with the crumbs that were left.

Saxon and Norman knights had ridden away in comradeship behind the glorious banners of King Richard, and gone to do battle in the Holy Lands. But the Normans left behind to rule England kept up the old tyranny. Prince John, Richard's brother, proved as barbaric as Richard was chivalric. He appointed men like the Sheriff of Nottingham and Guy of Gisborne: robber barons who sat in the great grey keeps of their granite castles and plotted to grow rich. They taxed and fined and robbed their Saxon subjects until starvation sat by every Saxon hearth. They dispossessed the poor who could not pay, the proud who would not pay, and anyone whose fortune they wanted for themselves.

Robin of Locksley, for instance, was cheated of his father's land by Gisborne. Where was the law to protect his rights, grant him justice? Gone to the Crusades with the King. Law and Justice no longer existed in the England ruled by Prince John.

Unless they lived on in Robin Hood.

That same cheated Robin of Locksley, to preserve his life, slipped away into the green forest and disappeared. Soon afterwards, a mysterious figure was glimpsed by travellers, dressed all in green, with green-feathered arrows in his quiver and green mosses streaking his cheeks. No one knew at first whether the "Man of Sherwood" truly existed or not. But then strange things began to happen.

Fat Norman merchants were robbed of their gold, and next day thin Saxon children found gold beneath their pillows. Cruel tax collectors were "relieved" of all their takings. Then money would fly in at the windows of widows, and flour fall like snow on starving villages. The mysterious Robin Hood was robbing the rich to feed the poor, and though the Norman soldiers hunted him like the hind, they could never find him. He had made the greenwood his own stronghold.

One by one, men persecuted or pursued by Norman law headed for the forest to join Robin Hood and to wear the "suit of green". They were outlaws to the Normans, but heroes to the Saxons. Their very existence burned like a green gleam in the imagination, a flame of hope.

"A tournament? Will there be archery?" asked Robin casually, waxing his bowstring with a stub of candle.

"That's the main event!" said Friar Tuck, tucking into his meal. "First prize is a golden arrow, presented by Gisborne himself." The Friar's words emerged speckled with breadcrumbs and flecks of fat. "Open to any archer in the land. The Prince himself is going to be there, so they say, the swine." Tuck was the only man in Robin's band not to wear the suit of green. In his brown habit, he could come and go to town unnoticed, unquestioned,

and bring them news, messages from wives and sweethearts, gifts from well-wishers. He was able, too, to deliver Robin's little "presents" to the poor of Nottingham.

Today his news was of a grand archery contest to be held within the castle walls. The outlaws, sitting around their campfire, greeted the news quietly, remembering other such festive holidays spent with their families.

"We know, without going, who's the best archer in England, don't we?" said Alan-a-Dale loyally, and all the outlaws shouted in one voice, *"Robin Hood!"*

"It would be pleasant to prove it, even so," murmured Robin.

"You *wouldn't*! You never would!" Much the Miller was horrified. "Tell him, Little John! Tell him it's too dangerous!"

"S'probably a trap," said Will Scarlett gloomily. "The Sheriff probably means to lure Robin inside the castle - thinks he won't be able to resist competing for a stupid golden arrow."

"Let's not disappoint him, then!" declared Robin, jumping to his feet.

There was a streak of recklessness in Robin which scared his Merrie Men. It was hard enough to keep alive in the inhospitable greenwood, without a man wilfully creeping into the stronghold of his worst enemy. And for what? An arrow of shiny gold that would not even fly?

The sun glinted on the golden arrow. The cushion it lay on was of blood-red velvet.

The castle grounds were bright with striped pavilions and painted flag-poles, the sky jagged with pennons. Tourney armour caught the sun and dazzled the eye. Chargers cloaked in cloth-of-gold stamped their hooves and jingled plumed bridles. It was a holiday in Nottingham and, for once, the brown and ragged townspeople were also allowed inside the castle precincts.

Entrants for the archery contest stood in a huddle: the best archers in Prince John's guard, the best archers in the Sheriff's employ, professional marksmen and amateur huntsmen. There were a few Saxons, too - arrowsmiths and bow-makers, for the most part. Impatiently they queued up to shoot at the distant butts.

Suddenly there was a flurry of excitement, as a young man in a green tunic was seized by castle guards and wrestled to the ground. "We knew you couldn't stay away, Robin Hood! Got you at last!"

But it was not Robin Hood at all, just a boy wearing green. Gisborne ground his teeth. He found archery tedious, and now he was obliged to sit through a whole afternoon of it.

Some arrows went wide, some buried themselves in the grass, ripping off their feather fletches. The butts looked like porcupines by the time all the bowmen had loosed their flights. Last of all, an old man, bent and bearded, shuffled to the firing line, carrying his arrows in a raffia basket. He began, with shaking hands, to fit an arrow to his bowstring.

"Get away, old man. Clear off!" they told him. "This is a young man's sport. Go home."

"All comers, it said," croaked the old man.

"He's holding up the competition! Get rid of him!"

"Oh, let him make a fool of himself. Takes less time than arguing."

The old man nodded and doddered, peered down the field at the butts as if he could barely see them, then feebly tugged back on his bowstring. The arrow plunged into the golden heart of the target.

"Fluke."

"Lucky!"

"Not half bad, Grandpa."

The competition continued, with everyone disqualified who did not hit gold. Round by round it became harder - the butts were moved farther off - and more bowmen were eliminated. But the luck of the old man held. The crowd began to warm to him: he was a ragged Saxon, after all. Every time he fired, they cheered. Every time a Norman missed, they cheered, too.

It came down to just three men: a Norman sergeant-at-arms, hand-picked by Guy of Gisborne, a pretty French knight in chequered velvet . . . and the old man, frail and lame, whose clothes had more holes in them than the canvas target. The butts were moved still farther off - so far now that they were scarcely in sight.

As the French knight took aim, a silly lady in the stands jumped up and waved to him for luck. It spoiled his concentration and the arrow went wide.

But the sergeant-at-arms fired the perfect shot. His arrow hit the gold dead centre. Even the Saxon crowds gasped with admiration and began to turn away. The contest was plainly over.

The old man congratulated the sergeant, who spat in his face and laughed. The nobles in the stand were rising and stretching themselves, stiff after so much sitting. The old man took a green-tipped arrow from his raffia basket and laid it to his bow. "I'll just see what I can manage," he quavered.

His arrow flew like a hornet. The thwack, as it hit canvas, sounded like an explosive charge. It pierced the selfsame hole as the sergeant's arrow, and dislodged it, leaving only one arrow thrumming with the force of impact.

"Did you see that?"

"Why? What happened?"

"He did it! Old Grandpa did it!"

The nobility milled about in their enclosure. As the old man approached, twisted and limping, to receive his prize, Prince John pointedly turned his back.

Guy of Gisborne picked up the golden arrow between finger and thumb and dropped it at the vagrant's feet. "You shoot quite well, old man," he said grudgingly, but there was no reply. He saw that the archer's face was turned not towards him but towards the Lady Marian. The mouth was hidden by the bird's nest beard, but the eyes were wrinkled with smiling. And the Lady Marian was smiling back!

"Well done, sir! Oh, well done!" she said.

"You are kind, beautiful maiden, past all my deserving," said the winner.

Now you ought to know that Sir Guy of Gisborne thought of the Lady Marian as his future bride (even though she did not care for the idea). He was furious to see her smiles wasted on a filthy, decrepit Saxon. He took hold of the shaggy beard to yank the rogue's head round to face him. The beard came away in his hand. The archer sank his teeth in Gisborne's clenched fist, then sprang backwards.

It was as if he had left his old age in Gisborne's grasp and been restored to youth. There stood a handsome youngster, straight-backed, bright-eyed and laughing.

"Robin Hood!" breathed Gisborne, and for a moment the two men looked at one another with bitterest hatred.

Then a voice in the crowd shouted, "Here, Robin! Over here!" A riderless horse, slapped on the rump, galloped towards the pavilion; Robin leapt into the saddle. The flying stirrups struck the faces of the guards who tried to stop him.

Gisborne was first to mount up and give chase, while Marian crammed her long plaits against her mouth and gazed after them. "Oh ride, Robin, ride!" she whispered under her breath. She alone among the spectators had recognized Robin Hood beneath his disguise - but then she was in love with him, and he with her.

The crowds scattered from in front of the galloping horses, as Gisborne pursued Robin towards the castle drawbridge. The golden arrow shone in Robin's hand. A cry rose spontaneously from the beggars and children by the gate: "Ride, Robin! Ride!"

But Gisborne was close behind, well mounted, and his sword out, whereas Robin's horse was a poor thing. His disguise allowed for no weapon: a longbow cannot be used in the saddle.

"I've a score to settle with you, you filth, you thief!" panted Gisborne, and the blade of his sword sliced the green feathers from Robin's arrows. "You've robbed my tax gatherers, stirred up the peasants, and thumbed your nose at me out of the greenwood tree! Well, now I'll show that scum of yours that their magic Robin Hood is nothing but common flesh and blood!" This time his blade shaved the hair from Robin's neck. They thundered over the castle drawbridge side by side.

"And I have a score of scores to settle with you, Gisborne!" panted Robin. "You robbed me of my father's land. You tread down the poor and make widows and orphans weep! You drove me to live like an animal in the greenwood . . ."

Gisborne swung, and Robin's hot blood flew back in his face, in his eyes.

"*... when everyone knows that you are the animal!*" Robin turned in the saddle and struck out, using the only weapon he had.

Watching from the castle yard, the crowds saw the two horses part. One went left, towards the forest, the other right, towards the town. It looked as if Gisborne had unaccountably turned aside and let Robin Hood escape.

A short while later, the bully's horse ambled down the streets of Nottingham town, reins dangling, foamy with sweat, hooves skidding on the cobbles. Shopkeepers and housewives, accustomed to the man's cruelty, drew back fearfully against the walls. Then one by one they stepped out again. They had seen the golden arrow shaft shining in the centre of Gisborne's crested surcoat, its point sunk deep in his heart. And they had seen death staring out of Gisborne's open eyes.

Greater tyrants remained, tyrants who made Gisborne seem like a gentleman. Until the true King of England returned, his subjects would continue to groan and suffer at the hands of Prince John and his robber barons. Only the existence of Robin Hood - out there - dressed like Spring among the greenwood trees - kept poor people from despair. The mere mention of Robin's name kept their hearts beating. The telling of his thousand daring exploits warmed them even when there was no fuel on the hearth. In the depths of a cruel winter, Robin was the green promise that Spring always returns.

# Brave Quest

A NATIVE AMERICAN MYTH

HE HAD nothing: no parents, no possessions, no position in the tribe but to be laughed at and scorned. Once, he had been handsome, but being handsome in deeds as well as face, he had tried to return a fallen eagle-chick to its nest and been gouged and gored by the parent birds. Now his face was hideously scarred, and though his name was Man-of-Little, everyone called him Scarface.

"Why don't you ask Marvellous-Girl to marry you?" they jeered. "You love her, don't you? What a perfect pair you'd make! The dove and the crow!" Their spite rained down on him sharp as arrows.

Of course he loved Marvellous-Girl: everyone did. Braves of every tribe for a hundred miles around came to ask for her in marriage. They all went away disappointed. How could Scarface even tread in the prints of her moccasins or pain her eyes with the sight of his ghastly face? If they had not goaded him, he never would have done so. But their cruelty stirred in him the dregs of an old pride, and he went to the lodge of Marvellous-Girl, and stood by the closed doorway.

"I love you, Marvellous-Girl. If a strong arm and a faithful heart can do you any service, take me for your husband. I stand at your door and sorrow, for what hope of love has a boy like me? But what love can do for you, I will do, for I am filled with love."

To his amazement, the woman inside did not shriek with laughter. The door flap lifted and her face appeared, as lovely as the new moon. "I can marry no one, Man-of-Little, but if I could, there is no one I would sooner have. For you are gentle and good, and your hair would be pleasing under my hand."

For a moment, Scarface could barely think. The face slipped out of sight, like the moon passing behind a cloud. "Why can you not marry?" he called, and the pigeons on the corn flew up in surprise.

"Because I am promised to the Sun."

"No!" He could hear her moving about inside the dark lodge, preparing a meal: the Sun's betrothed, the girl he loved. He bit back his jealousy. "You are greatly honoured, then."

Her rustling movements stopped. After a moment she said, "I would have felt more honoured, Man-of-Little, to be married to you."

Astonishment, like a fountain, leapt up within Scarface. "Then I'll shoot the Sun out of the sky!" he cried, and the vultures, picking over bones among the litter, took off in alarm.

"Shssh!" Her face appeared, lovelier than the moon. "Don't anger him. But you could go to the Sun's Lodge, if you dared, and beg him to release me. He might take pity on us. If he does, ask him to touch your face and heal that scar of yours. Then everyone will know he has renounced his claim and blesses our marriage."

"I'll go!" cried Scarface, and an eagle flying overhead heard him and dropped its prey.

Though he took food, the journey was so long that it was soon used up, and he lived on roots, berries and wild honey. Though he knew the paths to the east of the village, his journey was so long that he soon reached woodland paths he had never trodden before. Though he asked every person he met, "Where is the Sun's Lodge?", no one knew, and the journey was so long that he soon met with no more people. Instead he entered wild places inhabited only by animals.

Though he was young and strong, the journey was so long that at last he thought he could go no farther and sat down on a log. Polecat came trotting by, as black and white as snow on coal. "I am looking for the Sun's Lodge!" said Scarface to the Polecat.

"In all my life I have never seen it. But Bear is wise. Ask the Bear."

So Scarface searched out the Bear and found him scratching the bark from a tree, licking the insects from his paws. "I am looking for the Sun's Lodge," he said, quite fearless (for he had so little to lose that were the Bear to eat him, he would be little worse off).

"In all my days, I have never seen it," said Bear, "but Beaver goes where I cannot. Ask the Beaver."

So Scarface asked Beaver, who was building a lodge in the lake.

"In all my travels I have never seen the Sun's Lodge," said Beaver. "But Wolverine is cunning. Ask the Wolverine."

So Scarface searched out Wolverine, but by the time he found him, he was both famished and exhausted.

"The Sun's Lodge? Of course I know where it is," said the Wolverine. "But where is your canoe? You can hardly cross the Great Water without a canoe!"

"If that's where it is, I shall swim across!" declared Scarface. But that was before he saw, for the first time, the Great Salt Waters of the ocean, so vast that a man's life might be swum out amid its valleys and mountains. There

on the beach, Scarface sat down and wept tears as salt as the sea. He knelt back on his heels and addressed himself to the sky.

"Rightly was I named Man-of-Little at my birth, for I have neither the face nor the strength, nor the magic, nor the luck to make good of my life. Was it for nothing that I was born? I wish those eagles had eaten me, limb and life, rather than leave me here, on the shores of my shortcomings!"

A pair of eagles flying overhead heard him and swooped down. He raised his arms over his head, but he had no shield or weapon to fend them off.

The eagles' talons closed around his arms, and their beaks gripped his hair. Then, with a deafening clatter of wings, they lifted him - up and out over the ocean.

"There you are, young friend," they said, setting him down on the

farthermost shore. "We regret that our mistake has spoiled your life so far, but we do what we can in recompense. Follow that yellow path. It leads to the Lodge of the Sun."

With a whoop of joy, Scarface leapt along the path, his strength renewed, his hunger forgotten. Night had fallen, and he had only the moon to light his way. Presumably the Sun was indoors, sleeping in his lodge.

Just before dawn, he began to see, strewn along the path, various pieces of clothing and weaponry: a quiver of arrows with golden shafts, a headdress of white egret feathers, a gold spear, a tunic sewn with gilt thread, and moccasins of the softest kind. He stepped carefully over them, wondering at what kind of warrior owned such splendid things. Suddenly the leaves of a tree exploded overhead, and a youth plunged down on to his shoulders with a blood-curdling war-cry.

They rolled over and over together on the ground. Scarface easily broke free, but the young man did not seem much put out. "Why didn't you pick them up?" he asked breathlessly, putting on his tunic again and collecting up his possessions.

"All those beautiful things? Because they weren't mine," said Scarface.

"Pity. I could have challenged you to a fight for taking them - you must be out-of-the-ordinary honest, that's all I can say!" Scarface sat on the ground, winded and a little bewildered. "Oh! You don't know me, do you? I'm Morning Star, son of the Sun. He'd like you, my father. I make him angry, because I'm always doing what he tells me not to do. But he'd like you, I should think."

"I'm not so sure," said Scarface, with a wry smile. But Morning Star had already run off up the path.

"Let's go killing whooping cranes!" he called over his shoulder. "The Old Man says I mustn't - so it must be fun. Race you to the lake!"

Scarface got to his feet and ran after Morning Star. "If your father says you shouldn't, maybe you should respect the wisdom of his age!" His words came back at him, echoing off the shale sides of a valley dry but for a small lake glowing in the dawn. Around it, a flock of cranes sipped the water through long spiky beaks.

As Morning Star rushed at them, brandishing the golden spear, they rose up into the air - a clumsiness of bony wings and horny legs. Then they dropped down again, enveloping Morning Star in a blizzard of feathers. He gave one long, loud scream.

Without time to waste on fear, Scarface ran headlong into the storm of birds. Their long beaks were like tent pegs driven home with mallets. The leading edges of their wings were sharp as blades, and the clawed feet which kicked him were hoof-hard.

But with his fists alone, he bruised their scarlet beaks. With his bare hands he tore tail feathers from them in handfuls until they rose, squawking indignantly, and flapped away down the shale valley. Morning Star lay still along the ground, his body bleeding from a dozen wounds. Scarface

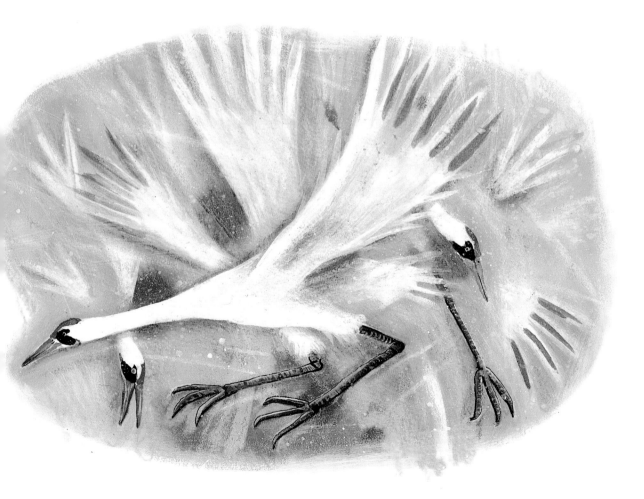

lifted him gently and carried him back to the yellow path and up to the door of the Sun's Lodge.

"What have you done?" demanded the fearful orange face which answered his knocking. It was blotched and marked in a hundred places by spots of old age. "Did you do this to him?"

Scarface could feel the hairs of his fringe frizzle, the lashes of his lids scorch. "He tried to go hunting whooping cranes by the lake in the valley. The birds mistook him for a foolish boy with too little respect for the advice of his father."

The heat of the Sun's fury cooled instantly, and he hurried Scarface indoors - into the largest and most magnificent lodge ever raised on a forest of poles. Scarface laid Morning Star on a heap of buffalo hides, fearing he must already be dead. But the merest caress of the old man's hand closed the wounds in Morning Star's body, and restored him to perfect health. So he was able to tell his father about meeting Scarface, about his out-of-the-ordinary honesty, about the whooping cranes blotting out his sky . . .

"You have saved my son's life," said the Sun solemnly. "How can I repay you?"

Once, twice Scarface opened his mutilated mouth to speak. But though courage had brought him through woodlands, over the ocean and up to the lodge door, he dared not speak. "You will destroy me where I stand, if I say the words in my heart."

"Are you not a guest in my lodge, and my son's best friend? . . . And Man-of-Little, do you think I don't recognize you? Do you think I don't glance down, once in a while, as I cross the sky each day? Do you think I don't listen, too? I was overhead in the sky the day you spoke to Marvellous-Girl at her door."

"Then touch my face and tell me I may marry her!" Scarface blurted.

The Sun reached out an elderly hand spotted as any leopard, and chucked Scarface under the chin like a little child. "Let me give you clothes and food for the journey," he said, "and water to wash yourself." As to Scarface's request, he said not a word.

It was not until Scarface looked down into the bowl of water which the Sun brought him, that he saw his face, perfect, restored, healed.

When Marvellous-Girl saw it, she reached out a hand too, through the doorway of her lodge, and touched his cheek. She did not even notice the quiver of golden arrows he was carrying, or the tunic sewn with gilt thread, or the headdress of egret feathers. "Tell the tribe's women to prepare for a wedding," she said. "Tomorrow, I think. At noon. When the Sun will be directly overhead."

They called their firstborn son Eagle, and the sons which followed after, Polecat, Beaver, Wolverine and Bear. But their daughter, of course, they named Woman-who-loves-Sunshine.

# Saving Time

## A POLYNESIAN MYTH

THE PACE of life is gentle on the sea-washed islands of Polynesia. Days are long and sunny, and no one hurries to get their work done or rushes a meal when it can be lingered over in the twilight.

It was not always so. Once, the People of the Islands rolled out of their beds at first light and scampered to their boats or to their plantations, dashed to do their work, never stopped to talk or sit - only to snatch a bite of food before the light failed.

"Quick, man, pick those coconuts while you can see which are ripe!"

"Quick, woman, beat that tree bark into cloth while you can see what you are beating!"

"Quick, child, find me bait for my fishing hook while you can still find the worm casts on the sand."

39

But many was the time that fishing canoes put out to sea in the morning only to lose sight of land in the failing light and go astray amid the night-dark waves. For the days were very, very short, the Sun speeding across the sky like a thrown ball, the daylight gone in the blinking of an eye.

One day, Maui sat in front of his family hut. The Sun had already set and only firelight illuminated his family's anxious faces as they gathered to eat the evening meal. Some of the food was spilled as the bowls were passed out; there was so little light to see by.

"This food's not cooked," complained a grandmother.

"I'm sorry. There wasn't time," said Maui's mother.

"There's nothing for it," said Maui, jumping up. "The day must be lengthened or how can we ever hope to get our work done between waking and sleeping?"

"Tell it to the Sun," grumbled some of the elders. "He rushes across the sky like a stone from a catapult and is gone in a twinkling."

"Then I must make him slow down!" said Maui confidently, and strode off along the beach.

First he fell over a turtle and then he fell over a canoe, for the moon was young and the beach was dark and Maui could barely see his hand in front of his face.

"What are you looking for?" called his sister, Hina.

"For a length of rope," Maui called back, peering around him without success.

"Don't you think you'd best wait till morning," suggested his sister, "when there's more light?"

In the morning, Maui found a length of rope made from coconut fibre and tied it in a noose. Then he walked to the eastern horizon (which took him the rest of the day), where a charred and gaping pit marked the spot at which the Sun leaps into the sky.

He circled the pit with the noose and, holding the other end of the rope, sat well back, through the long night, awaiting sunrise.

With a blinding, blazing bound, the Sun leapt out of his pit, hurtling towards his noonday zenith. The noose snapped shut around his shaggy head of flame - but the old Sun was moving so fast that the rope simply snapped like a spider's thread, and the great ball of fire never even noticed that he had been snared.

Maui returned home and, with the help of all the children, gathered up every coconut husk on every beach of every island. He stripped the hair shells and rolled the fibres into strands of coir. Then he plaited the fibres into a rope so strong he might have towed an island with it. He tied a noose in the rope and took it to the eastern horizon where, once again, he laid a snare to catch the rising Sun.

With one flaring, glaring bound, the Sun leapt into the sky and pelted towards his noonday zenith. The noose pulled tight around his shaggy head of flame - but no sooner did it touch the great heat of the incandescent Sun than it frizzled into flames, dropping away in a flurry of ash as the Sun hurried onwards.

The day was so short that by the time Maui reached home, it was already night-time again. He crept into the family hut and felt his way to where his sister Hina lay sleeping on her mat. With his sharp fishing knife, he cut off her long hair, purple-black with magic and as glossy as the night sea outside. Plaiting it into a rope, he made one last purple-black noose. By dawn, it was in place around the pit of sunrise.

With a whirling whoop of white fire the Sun leapt into the sky and flew towards his noonday zenith. But he was brought up short by the jerk of a snare. Hina's plaited hair closed tight around his throat, and he choked and struggled and thrashed about, kicking and scrabbling to break free.

"I will let you go on one condition!" shouted Maui, hanging on grimly to the end of the purple-black rope. "In future you must pass more slowly across the sky, so that the People of the Islands have a longer day, and can get their work done!"

The Sun rolled and spun, tugged and leapt, like a giant tunnyfish caught on a fishing line. But Maui was a great fisherman and he fought the Sun to a standstill. At last he hung panting in the air, great gouts of molten flame dropping like sweat from his golden face.

"I agree. I agree. From now, I shall creep across the sky as slowly as a turtle across a beach. Now let me loose." Maui loosened the noose of Hina's magic hair, and the Sun walked sedately towards his distant noonday zenith.

The days, after that, lasted from slow lilac dawn through leisurely golden hours and into a sunset as pink and orange as a reef of coral. At such times, when the People of the Islands linger over their meal and watch the beauty of the Sun's descent, they can still see some strands of Hina's hair caught in the Sun's corona, streaking the evening sky.

Of course, what the Sun does when finally he dives into his pit at the western horizon is entirely his own affair. Freed from his promise to Maui, he may soar and swoop, circle and somersault as fast as any turtle beneath the waves.

# The Lake that Flew Away

AN ESTONIAN LEGEND

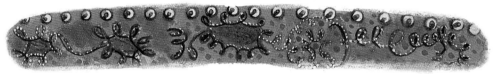

DO YOU suppose a lake has no feelings? No sense of pride? No self-esteem? Do you think that it can lie untended without suffering? Its weeds run riot, like unkempt hair; its fishes choke beneath the autumn leaves; its banks crumble under the feet of drinking cattle.

Lake Eim in Estonia is a vast tract of water a hundred fathoms deep. In the beginning, trees which seeded themselves around it drank its water and flourished, dense and leafy. A forest grew. So did the darkness within it. And soon, within the darkness of trees lurked a darkness of men.

Brigands and bandits made their lairs in the black entanglement of lakeside trees. They fished the lake for their suppers, and they spent long hours sprawled in drifting boats, dangling grappling hooks into the deeps. For it was rumoured the lake held great treasures from an earlier civilization.

The men did not dredge the shallows, or clear the weed, or cut back the nettles that mustered at the waterside. That would have been hard work, and they had forsworn hard work.

So why did their pockets jingle with gold, and their gambling last all night? Because each time a traveller passed through the wood - a pilgrim or a merchant - they cut his throat and threw his body in the deep, dark waters. The blood stained Lake Eim. The blood shamed Lake Eim. Red blood stained the bankside flowers and dripped from the bending grasses on to the face of the lake. The blood soured and fouled the still waters of the lake, till it shivered with a hundred cat's-paws, even on a windless day.

In horror and disgust, the lake seethed, and bubbles of marsh gas rose from the rotting weed on its bed. "I will not be stained with the sin of these wicked men. I shall leave this place!"

The Robber Chief, stirring in his sleep, heard the slap-slap of water on the lake shore. He heard a *suck-shuck* as of mud parting company from a boot or a boat. Drops of water fell on the roof, and he thought, "Rain," and turned over to sleep again.

Suddenly, hands were pulling at the covers and voices shouting in his ear: "Come quick! Come quick! The lake is . . . well, it's . . . the lake, it's . . ."

"The lake is what?" demanded the Robber Chief, grabbing a bandit by the throat. "What is the lake doing, that you wake me in the middle of the night?"

"Flying away, Chief!"

"Flying away." The Robber Chief pulled the blankets over his head and cursed his cronies, body and soul.

"It's true, Chief!"

"Like a carpet, Chief!"

"Up and away, Chief, all silver and glittering!"

The Robber Chief rolled out of bed and stumbled to the window. Over-head in the sky hung a billion gallons of water, shining like metal plate, thick as cumulus clouds, spreading out to all points of the compass, a translucent ceiling. If it were to fall . . .

The bandits stood stock still, waiting for a billion steely gallons to fall on their heads like the end of the world. Minute after minute they listened to the gentle hiss of moving water cascading through the sky. Then the moon bobbed into view again, like a fishing float, and the danger was past.

"Well? What are you waiting for?" bellowed the Robber Chief. "Get out there and make the most of it! There'll be fish by the barrel-load, too, there for the picking up! And treasure! Don't forget the treasure! All there for the taking!"

As they pelted down to the lake, dawn was just rising.

"The boats have gone, Chief!"

"Who needs 'em? We can walk!"

They plunged on, up to their knees in mud. The lake bed was certainly alive with wriggling movement. And treasure chests lay about, smashed open at the hinges and steaming in the early sun.

A bandit thrust his arm into one of the chests, then drew it out with a shriek. The chest was full of frogs! Another was full of water snakes, another lizards. Not a fish, not a single bearded barbel or dappled trout lay stranded by the lake's departure. But every lizard, reptile, newt, salamander, frog and slug that had lived in the mud of the lake was crawling now towards the shore.

The brigands shrank back in revulsion - only to see the nasty slimy livestock of the lake crawl past into their dens, into their beds, into their boots and bags and hats.

They burned everything - their lairs and all they had stolen. They razed the forest to its stumps, then trudged away, their wicked lives in ashes, leaving an empty crater encircled by fire.

Meanwhile, Lake Eim carried its careful burden of fish and treasure through the sky. It flew so high that people below looked up and said, "What cloud is that hiding the sun?" Hunters looked up and said, "What flock of birds is that blacking out the sun?"

Then the lake came to a land parched and cracked, brown and destitute for want of water. The poor peasants there held out their hands, hoping the cloud might spare them a few drops of meagre rain. Then suddenly, out of the sky it swooped - a sluicing wealth of water, which seemed to glitter with jewels.

"Make me a bed to lie in, and I shall stay with you," offered Lake Eim, in a voice like a thundering waterfall.

The peasants snatched up their hoes and spades. The children dug with their hands; the women wheeled away the dry earth in barrows. Inside a week they made a bed for the lake, and Eim settled into it, with a sound like a weary groan. Fish danced on their tails on the surface, while each circular ripple to spread from the centre to the shore washed up a trinket of gold or a few silver coins. Several little boats bobbed about, too, on the choppy waves.

First the peasants thanked God, with prayers in the church. Then they thanked the lake, with flowers that they floated on its face. They planted willow trees and dug cattle troughs, made osier beds in the shallows, and built jetties out from the shore. They channelled water to their fields, and the fields flourished. They built a town and fed it on fish, and the town flourished. (All the fish fry they returned, so that the fish stocks thrived.) In short, they cared for the lake, and the lake cared for them.

Which is as it should be.

If you don't want your bed full of newts.

# Admirable Hare

A LEGEND FROM CEYLON

FOR A FEW brief years, the ruler of the skies lived on earth as Prince
Siddhartha, who was later called Buddha when he became wiser than any
other man. But just once, they say, he met an animal whose kindness was
an example and a marvel, even to the gods.

One night, the Buddha, who lived as a wandering hermit, got lost in a
forest in Ceylon. The dense canopy of leaves overhead obscured the guid-
ing stars. The smooth, blank moon poured its light only into the forest
clearings, like milk into cups. In one of these clearings, the Buddha met a
hare called Sasa.

"Your face is the face of a good man," said the hare, "but your expression
is that of a man who has lost his way."

"True, my velvet-eared friend," admitted the Buddha. "I am lost."

"Then permit me to guide you to the edge of the forest."

"I'm afraid I have no money to repay such kindness," said the Buddha, thinking that perhaps the hare earned a living in this way.

"Sir," replied Sasa, bowing gracefully from his slender hips, "the debt would be all mine, if you would allow me to help you on your way, and share conversation with me as we go."

So the Buddha was steered through the wood by this most charming hare, and as they walked, they talked. Sasa was hungry for any wisdom the Buddha could spare him. The Buddha was simply hungry, but did not say so.

At the edge of the wood, Sasa said, "I know this meagre forest and how long you have been lost in it. You must be very hungry."

"You are indeed shrewd in judgement, my velvet-skinned friend," replied the Buddha. "I'm famished."

The hare sat back on his heels. "That will not do. Indeed, it will not. Please do me the honour of skinning and eating me. I am reasonably plump, as you can see, and too young for my meat to be tough. Here - I'll build you a fire so that you can cook me."

Leaving the Buddha no chance to protest, Sasa dashed to and fro, gathering firewood into a heap which he lit with the spark from two stones. "Thank you for teaching me so much of which I was ignorant," said the hare, bowing once more from his slender hips. "Enjoy your meal." And with that, he leapt into the flames.

With the speed of a hawk, the Buddha's hand shot out and caught Sasa by his long velvet ears. Once, twice he swung the creature around, then threw him upwards, upwards. The hare smashed through the spreading canopy of a tree, and leaves and twigs rained down on to the Buddha's upturned face. But Sasa kept on flying, upwards, upwards, until he hit the very face of the moon.

"Such a generous creature shall not die - no, never!" the Buddha called after him. "In future, let the world look up at night and see my friend, Sasa-in-the-Moon, and remember how noble a creature he was, and how kind to a penniless hermit!"

For though he was Buddha-in-the-Wood, with no bite of food to call his own, he was also Buddha, Ruler-of-the-Skies, and had only to reach out a hand to fulfil his every wish.

Sasa lived on in the moon - you can see the happy shape of him dancing. Many a traveller lost at night has looked up and found encouragement in seeing him there.

# All Roads Lead to Wales

THE COUNTRYSIDE of Europe is struck through with roads as straight as if they were drawn on the map with a ruler. Though some have been broken by frosts, and weeds have grown through the cracks, and mud has buried them from sight, still they are there, just below the surface, like the main arteries of the land, bearing blood to its heart. This is a story told by men who found the roads and wondered at their marvellous straightness and excellent construction, wondered at the men who had built them and then disappeared without trace from the ruined villas nearby.

Maximus was Emperor of Rome, and no one was more fit to be so. The known world paid him homage and its merchants met in his market places. When he hunted, it was in the company of great men, and when he

52

hunted that day, thirty-two kings rode in his party.

The heat of the day made the landscape quake. The dogs yelped away into the distance. Sleep rose up from the ground mixed with the dust from his mare's hooves, and cloaked Maximus in weariness. He lay down on a grassy river bank, and his centurions made a shelter of their shields to ward off the sun's heat. Beneath his dark shell, Maximus slept, and while he slept he dreamed - a dream so vivid that the events of the morning grew gauzy and unreal.

He flew along a river in his dream, or leaned so far over the prow of a ship that he saw only the water speeding below him. Upstream he sped, towards the source of the river, higher and higher till he came at last to a mountain - surely the highest in the world. Crossing the peak, he found another river issuing from the far side. He followed it down through the foothills, through fields and forests to its estuary and the sea. At the mouth of the river stood a city, its houses clinging to the skirts of a castle with towers of yellow and green and grey. At the foot of the castle wall, the sea rocked a fleet larger than all the navies of Rome. One ship in particular drew his eye, for its planks were alternately gold and silver and its gangway was a bridge of ivory.

Maximus, in his dream, crossed the ivory bridge just as the silk sail of the gilt and silver ship filled and billowed in his face. The ship carried him over sea lanes and obscure oceans to an island more beautiful than any he had ever seen. Still a strange curiosity carried him onwards, across the island from coast to coast, where he found the far side more lovely yet. Though its mountains were clad in mist, and tressed with rain, its valleys were fleecy with sheep and the river he followed was chased with silver spray. Once again, it was at the river's mouth that his dream brought him to a castle; inside the castle to a hall; inside the hall to a table. There it set him down.

Two princes were playing chess, while an old king sat nearby carving more chess pieces: knights and bishops and pawns. He looked up at Maximus, but a girl seated beside him was quicker in getting to her feet. Her hair, circled with gold, lifted and blew as she beckoned for Maximus to

sit beside her in a chair of red gold. Thigh against thigh, arm against arm, hand against hand they sat. Then the Princess rested her cheek against his, turned her face towards him, smiled and offered him her mouth to ...

A baying of hounds, a blare of horns, a thudding of hooves, and the shell of shields over the Emperor's head fractured and let in the sunlight. "Your Majesty? Are you well? Such a very long sleep in the middle of the day! Perhaps the heat ..." The sunlight and noise washed away the dream, the joy, the face of his beloved princess. Maximus awoke with a cry like a man stung by wasps, and clutched his hands to his heart. His hounds tumbled round him, and thirty-two kings stared.

On the way back to the palace, Maximus said not a word, and for a whole week afterwards would neither eat nor sleep, speak nor leave his room. It was as though, with the ending of the dream, he had breathed out a breath and could not draw the next. Physicians whispered outside his door. Rumours spread through the city that melancholy had conquered the invincible Maximus, and the thirty-two kings murmured among themselves.

Suddenly Maximus burst from his room: "Summon my three finest men and saddle the best horses in Rome!"

He sent the three out into the three divisions of the earth, to search for the pieces of his dream: the country, the river, the castle, the two young Princes, the daughter, the King. He described every detail of his dream and said, "Look, and do not stop looking until three years of looking have found nothing! For this dream went out of me like blood from a wound, and I fear my life depends on finding that place, that woman, that kiss."

The three messengers departed into the three divisions of the earth, and each found islands, and each found rivers, each found castles and each found kings within them. But of the beautiful country of Maximus's dream - nothing.

They came home forlorn and fearful, and found the Emperor a shrunken man, like a sail emptied of wind. Rebellion was stirring in thirty-two dark corners of the Empire, because Maximus cared too little to put it down. "I shall never see her again, and I left my heart in her keeping," was all he said.

Then one of the messengers said, "Master, won't you go yourself and look for the pieces of your dream? For the dream was sent to you and not to us!" It was so insolent a thing to say that the messenger trembled with fright. Maximus lifted his head and parted the fingers which covered his scowling eyes.

"Wise man!" he cried. "What you say is true!"

Putting on his hunting clothes once more, he took the selfsame mare from the stables, then rode into the green hills, allowing the horse to ramble and amble, on tracks and off. When she grew thirsty, the mare stopped by the banks of a river, and Maximus dismounted too and bent to drink.

"I have been here before," he said, all of a sudden, as the water raced by beneath his breast. "This is the river of my dream!"

This time he commissioned thirteen messengers to follow the river upstream to its source. "Let each man stitch to his cape a sleeve of gold, so that whatever country he comes to, there he shall be recognized as a messenger of Maximus, Emperor of the Romans! I would go myself, but I have rebellions to quell!" The Emperor seemed quite his old self again.

The thirteen messengers followed the river till they reached its source high in the highest mountain they had ever seen. They followed the river which plunged down from the peak and wandered through a dozen countries to the sea. There they found a city and a castle with turrets of yellow, green and grey, a fleet of ships, and a gangplank of walrus ivory. Crossing over it, they took ship on a galleon clinkered with silver and gold.

"...Everything was just as you said, master!" they reported back a hundred days later. Their golden sleeves were caked with sea salt and dust, but their eyes shone brighter than gold. "In a hall, in a castle held in the arms of a river, we saw an old man carving chess pieces, and two boys playing nearby. And there in the centre of the room was a maiden in a chair of red gold!"

"Did you speak? Did you ask her name?" Maximus scarcely dared to hear them out.

"We did as you commanded us, and fell on our knees before her and said, 'Hail Empress of Rome,' and told her your story from sleeping to waking."

Maximus was as pale as death. "What did she say?"

" 'Sir,' she said, 'I don't doubt what you tell me. But if the Emperor loves me, let him come here and fetch me himself. My name is Elen.' "

After that, Rome stirred like a man waking. The army streamed out of their barracks; the shopkeepers swarmed to the palace with supplies; the ladies waved kerchiefs from their windows, and chariots clashed broadside in the gates. The whole might of Rome galloped northwards, northwards and west - across the Alps, across the fields of France. They reached the sea at the castled coast, and took ship for Britain. And every step of the way, Maximus said, "It is just as I saw in my dream!"

Without pause, Maximus pressed on westward, through the difficult green confusion of Britain's ancient forests until at last he came to Wales. And there, on the farthest shore, amid mountains clad in mist and streams chased with silver spray, he found the castle of King Eudaf.

The Princes Cynan and Adeon sat playing chess, while their father carved new pieces: knights and bishops and pawns. And there, in the centre of the room, in a chair of red gold, sat the Princess Elen.

Into her arms rushed Maximus, and held her close, as though they were lovers who had been kept apart for too long. They married next day.

So dear was Elen to Maximus (and he to her) that he stayed seven years and could not bring himself to leave. His name was reshaped by the minstrels into Maxen, and his nature reshaped into a man of the valleys, where song and poetry are more important than politics or war.

But after seven years, word came from Rome - from a usurper who had filled Maxen's place and wore his imperial crown. *'Since you have been gone seven years,'* he wrote, *'you forfeit the right to call yourself Emperor of the Romans.'*

Then Maxen stirred himself out of his lover's dream, and rode and

sailed and climbed and marched back to Rome, to conquer it in the name of Elen. And there he stayed, pruning back the weeds which had overgrown the Empire during seven years of neglect.

Meanwhile, Elen gave orders for straight and sturdy roads to be built across all Italy and Gaul, across Britain and into Wales, so that a man might come and go along them at the speed of a galloping horse, from the centre of the world to the most beautiful corner of the Empire. Felling forests and quarrying hills, fording rivers and draining bogs, her road builders laid down hardcore and clinker, slabs and kerbs, never going round an obstacle but removing it utterly with pick and spade and brute force, letting nothing stand in their way.

These are the roads which the frosts chipped, the weeds invaded, the mud washed out. But they were built so true, so deep-founded, so straight, that they still cross the landscape like ruled lines.

To and fro rode Maxen of Rome, to and fro between the centre of the world and the most beautiful corner of his empire - even in summer's heat, or winter's muddy flood. And all so that he might sleep in the arms of Elen, a dreamless, blissful sleep.

# Rainbow Snake

IN DREAMTIME, our ancestors walked the Song Lines of the Earth, and thought about us, though we did not even exist. The Earth they walked was a brown flatness, its only features a few humpy huts built to keep off the sun, the dark, monsters and falling stars. Little tribes of people talked together in their own languages, and sometimes got up and danced their own magic dances. But even magic in those days was brown, drab and unremarkable, for there were no colours to conjure with.

The only colours shone in the sky. Sometimes, after a storm, as rain gave way to sun, a distillation of colours hung in the air, spanning Australia: the Rainbow. And that rainbow, like the people below it, dreamed, thought and had longings in its heart. "I will go down," it thought, "and find a tribe of people who think as I think, and dance as I dance, and we shall enjoy each other's company."

So the Rainbow drank all its own magic, and writhed into life. Whereas before it had been made only of falling rain and sunlight, each raindrop turned into a scale and each glimmer into a sinew of muscle. In short, it transformed itself into a snake. Twisting and flexing, its body a blaze of colour, it snaked its way down the sky to the edge of the Earth. Its jaws were red, its tail violet, and in between, its overlapping scales passed through every other shade.

But the Rainbow Snake was massively heavy. As it slithered along, it carved a trench through the featureless countryside, and threw aside mounds of mud. Because it was so huge, the trenches were valleys, and the mounds mountains. The next rain which fell was channelled into rivers, and puddling pools, so that already the world was altered by the presence of the Snake.

Rainbow Snake travelled from the Bamaga Point southwards through the bush, and every now and then raised its scarlet head and tasted the air with its flickering tongue. It listened too, with its lobeless ears. Sometimes it heard voices, but did not understand them. Sometimes it heard music, but the music moved it neither to tears nor laughter. "These are not my kind of people," it thought, and went on southwards, always south.

Then one day, it found a happy, laughing people whose language it partly understood and whose music made it sway - rear and sway, sway and dance - to the rhythm of the didgeridoo.

The dancing faltered. The dancers froze. The music died away. For towering high above them, jaws agape, the people saw a gigantic snake with scales of every colour in the rainbow. Its eyes closed in rapture, it swayed its sinuous body in time to the music.

When the music fell silent, it opened its gigantic eyes and looked down at them. Mothers drew their children close. Warriors fingered their spears. The Snake opened its mouth . . .

"I am Rainbow Snake, and you are my kin, for you speak the same language I think in, and make the music I have heard in my dreams."

An elder of the tribe, still balanced on one foot in mid-dance, looked up from under his hand. His bright teeth shone as his face broke into a smile. "In that case, you're welcome, friend! Lay yourself down and rest, or lift yourself up and dance - but don't let's waste another moment's fun!" The people gave a great shout of welcome, and went back to feasting.

Next day, Rainbow Snake coiled itself round the village, and sheltered it from the wind. Its flanks shaped the land during daylight hours, and in the evening it ate and drank and talked with the villagers. It was a happy time. Even afterwards, it was remembered as a happy time.

After all its travels, the Snake knew more dances than the people did, and from its place in the sky, it had seen more wonders. It taught them all it knew, and in honour of Rainbow Snake, the people decorated their bodies with feathers and patterned their skin, as the snake was patterned (though in plain, stark white).

Then it happened, the terrible mistake.

Dozing one night, mouth wide open, Rainbow Snake felt the pleasant tickle of rain trickling down its back and splashing in its nostrils. The patter of something sweet on its rolled tongue it mistook for rain, and closed its mouth and swallowed. Too late, it realized that the shapes in its mouth were solid.

Two boys, looking for shelter from the rain, had mistaken the Snake's huge mouth for a cave and crept inside. Now they were deep in its coiling stomach, and the Snake could not fetch them back. What to do?

Keep silent and hope the boys were not missed? No. The tribe were certain to notice, and would guess what had become of the lost boys. Admit to eating them, and listen to the mothers weep and reproach it? No. Better to slip away noiselessly, forgoing old friends and seeking out new ones.

Away it went, slithering silently, slowly and sleepily away over the wet ground, colourless in the starlight. It wrapped itself around Bora-bunara Mountain and slept.

Waking to find Rainbow Snake gone and the two boys lost, the tribe did indeed guess what had happened. They did not shrug their shoulders and they did not sit down and weep. Instead, they grabbed their spears and hollered, *"Murder!"* Then they followed the Snake's tracks, plain to see in the wet earth. They sped along the valley carved by its leaving, and had no difficulty in finding its resting place on the peak of Bora-bunara.

The Snake's dreams were pleasant and deep. Its stomach was full, and its contented snores rolled like thunder down every side of the mountain. Boulders tumbled, and shale cascaded, making a climb treacherous. But three brothers clambered nimbly up the rocky escarpments, knives clenched in their teeth. They slit open the side of Rainbow Snake; scales fell in a rain of indigo, green and blue. They opened the wound and shouted inside to the boys . . .

But the great magic of which the Snake was made had part-digested the children. Out past the rescuers fluttered - not boys, but two brightly

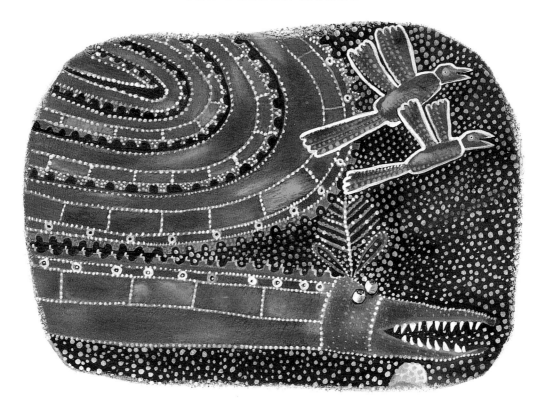

coloured birds. Their plumage was indigo, green and blue. Soaring high in the sky, they circled the mountain twice, then flew off, singing joyfully in the language of the birds.

The three brothers looked at one another and shrugged. Why grieve for boys who have been turned into birds? Their story has ended happily, after all. Only when they turned to make their descent did they see their friends and neighbours at the bottom of the mountain, jumping, gesticulating and pointing up at the Snake.

The Snake had opened its eyes.

Feeling a pain in its side like a stitch, the Rainbow Snake experienced a sudden draughty coldness in its stomach. It felt, too, a leaking away of its magic, like blood. And worst of all, it felt *betrayed*.

"I knew my little mistake might end our friendship," it hissed, "but I never realized it would stir you up to such *insolence*! Attack the Rainbow Spirit? Cut open your benefactor? Shed the scales of a Sky Creature? I'm hungrier now than I was before. And how do you think I shall satisfy that hunger, eh? I know! *I'LL EAT YOU, EVERY ONE!*"

The tongue which darted from its mouth was forked lightning. Its tail drummed up thunder. It crushed the mountain like bread into breadcrumbs, and thrashed the outback inside out and back to front.

In their terror, some people froze, some ran. Some even escaped. Some wanted so much to get away that they ran on all fours and wore down their legs to the thinness of jumbuck. Some leapt so far and so high that they turned into kangaroos. Some, in hiding under rocks, became tortoises and turtles. Others, who stood stock-still with fright, put down roots and turned into trees; others climbed them and turned into koala with big frightened eyes. Some leapt off Bora-bunara and flew away as birds. And some burrowed deep and became platypuses.

To escape the rampage of venomous Rainbow Snake, they became anything and everything, transforming the landscape almost as much as the angry serpent was doing with its lashing tail.

At last Rainbow Snake exhausted itself and, leaving behind a trail of destruction, hurled itself headlong into the sea. Through the half-circle of the setting sun it slithered, like an eel swallowed down the world's throat.

And next morning, it was back in place again, as though it had never left: the Rainbow, spanning the sky like a breath of peace: a miasma of rain and sunlight, a trick of the light. A reminder of stormy nights.

But when the airy Rainbow Spirit looked down on the Earth below, the landscape it saw was transformed. So too were the lives of our ancestors, for some were animals and some were plants, and those who were still men and women were wiser men and women by far.

# Juno's Roman Geese

A ROMAN LEGEND

VEII WAS an Etruscan city, a place of rumour and legend, full of treasure. At the very height of the Roman Empire, Rome set its sights on conquering Veii, but for ten years it stood besieged but unconquered. Camillus, commander of the Roman army, wanted to capture it more than anyone, wanted it more than anything. He fell on his face before the altars of the gods and prayed for success. And he wondered how to enter a city which for ten years had kept out all attackers.

"I shall not enter by force, but by subtlety, silently and in secret," he thought. Then he summoned his engineers and showed them a plan of the city. "If we were to dig a tunnel under the walls, here, and bring it out here, by the temple of Juno . . ."

Night and day they dug, passing the loose earth back down the passage.

Like moles they tunnelled, silent, and black with Etruscan dirt, working in pitch darkness. Then one evening, the soil gave way to something hard. Camillus wormed his way along the narrow tunnel. He stroked the smooth marble overhead with his fingertips. "We have come up right *under* the temple of Juno," he whispered.

So after dark, when no footfall came from overhead, Camillus raised a paving stone and peered about. The dark temple was a vast echoing hollow. He felt like a sailor in the stomach of a whale. He felt, too, as if he were being watched. Camillus looked up, looked higher, and drew a gasp of breath. For looking down at him was the monumental figure of the goddess Juno. Seven metres tall, and clad in slightly ragged, rather grubby cotton robes, her eyes looked directly into his. Scraps of litter blew across the temple floor.

"Phew! Only a statue," he might have said. But he did not. He took off his helmet, stood to attention, and saluted the Queen of the Gods. His lips moved in silent prayer. "Oh Juno, prosper me this night, and I shall give you a temple finer than this, filled with the scent of burning herbs, and I shall people it with white geese, so that you never stand lonely in the small hours of the night."

The white marble face looked down impassively, an artefact carved by human hands, nothing more. And yet the clothing blowing round her lent an impression of movement.

"On, men," whispered Camillus. "The city of Veii is ours, if the gods are with us tonight!"

One by one, the Romans crawled through the black tunnel and out into Juno's temple. It stood at the centre of the city, so that when they burst out - like adders hatching from a white egg - the city was stung at its very heart, and fell with barely a cry.

Next day, a queue of wagons stood in the market place. The treasures of Veii were being loaded for transportation to Rome. Statues reclined awkwardly in straw-lined carts - even pillars and mosaics were being loaded: everything beautiful, everything deserving of admiration was carefully stowed and driven away.

But inside the temple of Juno, there was a problem. Camillus went to investigate and found his troops standing stock-still round the statue of Juno. "What's the matter?"

The troops were tongue-tied, embarrassed. "We were washing her, right, sir? Bathing her, like you told us, sir, and dressing her in new clothes. Suddenly - now, don't be angry, sir . . ."

"Suddenly what?"

"Suddenly she seemed too . . . too *holy* somehow. We're all afraid to touch her, sir."

Camillus was not angry. He too had felt the aura of holiness which surrounded the great statue of the Queen of Heaven. Instead of shouting at the men to get on with their work, he took off his plumed helmet, bowed to the statue and called, "Juno! Great Queen of all the gods! Is it your wish to go to Rome?"

The men stared, transfixed. The horses harnessed to the cart at the temple door trembled in their shafts. Then they saw it - everyone saw it: a serene nod of the marble head, the merest closing of the eyes in affirmation. "I am content," said the gesture. "You may take me now."

Camillus was as good as his word. He did not rest until Juno was ensconced in the finest temple on Capitoline Hill, her shrine decorated with flowers, and the gardens round about busy with Roman geese. Waddling to and fro, toes turned in and hips wagging, the birds made a comical priesthood. But geese are the sacred birds of Juno, and their honking rang out piercingly, reminding the Romans daily to worship the Queen of Heaven.

Rome gobbled up the treasures of Veii and lauded the heroic victor Camillus, carved his statue, and made speeches of thanks to him in the Senate . . . then they put war behind them, preferring peace.

Once, the Romans had looked towards Veii and thought, "We wish to have its treasure for our own." But the conquest of Veii and more such cities made Rome herself a treasure-house. Soon others were looking at Rome with hungry eyes and saying, "We wish to have its treasure for our own."

One day, a voice was heard in the streets of Rome. At first the people mistook it for the honking of Juno's geese, but it became more plain - deep and mellifluous, but still, perhaps, a woman's voice ... It woke them from their sleep. It made the night watch shiver. "Prepare, Rome, beware! The Gauls are coming!"

The Gauls? It was laughable. The Gauls were uncultured barbarians who painted their half-naked bodies and wore animal skins. They had no system of government, no great cities, no drama or literature, no education, no empire. Hardly a civilization to be reckoned with, in comparison with the might of Rome! Camillus might have told them to pay more heed to the voice, but Camillus had been banished to the provinces - a man of war put out to grass.

When the Gauls came, they came like beasts, without strategies or cunning, but with brute force. What they fought, they killed. What they captured, they destroyed. Like fire across stubble they came, and all the fine words in the world could not stop them reaching the gates of Rome.

"Where is Camillus to defend us?"

"Gone to the country! Banished to Ardea!"

"Where are the gods to help us?"

"They shouted in the streets, but we wouldn't listen. Too late now! Run! Hide! The Gauls are at the gates!"

Some Romans ran away into the vine-strewn countryside and hid. Those who were fit enough ran with armfuls of belongings for Capitoline Hill. The hill was the city's natural keep - a high, unassailable crag adorned with white temples and glimmering now in the orange light of fires down below. Like surf over a pebble beach, the barbarians, as they pillaged Rome, left no stone where it had lain before. For sheer love of destruction, they pulled the lovely city down round their own ears, for they placed no value on its beauty, found nothing admirable, coveted nothing but blood and terror and death.

Like the sea also, they reached a point beyond which they could not go, for Capitoline Hill could be climbed only by a narrow path, and the besieged Romans could pick off an approaching enemy with ease.

"We have only to wait for you to starve!" bawled the barbarians in their guttural, shapeless language. Then they set about roasting the horses they had slaughtered, and feasting at the foot of the hill. High above them, the Romans watched the fires consume their beloved city, until the heat dried their eyeballs and left them no longer able to cry. Then they wrapped themselves in their cloaks and went to sleep, watched over by the beautiful white statues of their gods.

"Give them time to doze off," said the barbarian chieftain, gnawing on a hock bone, "then we'll finish them. Smash their gods and burn their temples." Beside him, face down on a shattered mosaic floor, a Roman traitor lay amid a pool of bloodstained gold. He had sought to make his fortune by betraying a secret path up Capitoline Hill. The Gauls had taken his information, then cut his throat. Now nothing stood between them and the remnants of Rome.

In the darkest time of night (as when Camillus had burrowed under the walls of Veii), the Gauls crawled and scrambled up the side of Capitoline Hill, daggers in their teeth and rags around their swords to keep metal from clanking against rock. The Romans generally fought their battles by day, after grand speeches, cleansed by prayer, in full sight of the sun. But the Gauls came creeping, sneaking, worming their way up the precipitous path, to slit throats under cover of dark.

At the foot of Juno's statue, the sacred geese fussed and fretted. Their big feet paddled across the chequered floor with a *plash plash plash*.

Hand over hand came the Gauls. Nearly there now. Mouths full of filthy curses, the blood lust rising. An arm over the low wall of a terrace, a knee, a cautious lifting of one eye . . .

*"Haaaaaarkhkh! Haaaaaarkhkh!"*

They were met by orange jabs of pain. Hard white wings beat at their eardrums, and huge black feet, hard as bone, paddled on their upturned faces. Geese!

With pecks and kicks, the geese dislodged the first attackers, then their honking woke the sleeping Romans. *"Haaaarkhkh! Haaaarkhkh!"* It was louder than braying donkeys. One Gaul, in falling, dislodged others: an avalanche of Gauls. Beakfuls of hair sprinkled the marble terraces.

Once awake, the besieged men and women fought with all the valour of true Romans. Morning found the Gauls licking their wounds like kicked dogs, and bemoaning the "winged monsters" which had beset them in the dark. They would make no more night-time assaults on Capitoline Hill. Besides, the Romans were now on their guard against sneak attacks. And within the week, the cry went up from the roof of Juno's temple, "Camillus! Camillus is coming!"

Camillus came in behind the Gauls and, scouring them out of the fire-blackened ruins of Rome, drove them into the Tiber. He dealt with them as a man might an infestation of woodlice. And although the destruction left behind was terrible, still forests do grow again after forest fires. In fact, they grow more vigorous and green and beautiful than before.

As for the geese, they were declared heroes and heroines of the battle, crowned with laurel and feted with corn. They fretted and fussed about, like old aunts embarrassed by overmuch attention. But it seemed to Camillus, as he sprinkled corn from a silver pan, that Juno looked on with an expression of pride. Their honking was a note more self-important, too. "Make way for Juno's geese," they seemed to say. "Make way for Juno's *Roman* geese! We saved *her* temple! We saved *her* city!"

# John Barleycorn

AN AMERICAN MYTH

NO SOONER did they lay eyes on him than the men of the farms decided to kill John Barleycorn. Though he had never done them harm, Farmer Mick and Farmer Mack, Farmer Mock and Farmer Muck ganged up on him in broad daylight and tumbled him to the ground. They dug a hole and buried his body in a field, and though the rooks flapped out of the tree-tops and circled overhead, no one else witnessed the dreadful crime.

Fingers and faces numbed by the raw cold, the four assassins trudged silently to the inn and, beside a log fire, tried to warm their hands round tankards of cold water. April rain spattered the windows, and the rookeries in the treetops faded from sight as the afternoon sky grew dark.

The way home took Farmer Mick past the field where John Barleycorn lay buried, but it was too dark to see the place where the clods of earth were piled on his yellow head.

The days grew longer and the sun warmer. Farmer Mick and Farmer Mack, Farmer Mock and Farmer Muck often drank water together at the local inn. They were kept busy milking and lambing, while their wives made butter and skimmed cream off the bowls in the dairy. None of them saw what the rooks saw from high in the trees - a single sharp green finger poking out between the clods, a long, reaching arm ...

Then one evening, Farmer Mick stumbled into the inn, breathless, pointing back the way he had come. "Have you seen? Have you seen? John Barleycorn's up again!"

Their arms slung round each others' necks, the farmers peered out through the low dirty window. "Ach, he's nought but a green boy. We'd be wasting our time to chase after him!" And they settled to a game of skittles instead.

One particularly sunny day, however, as Farmer Mick walked down to the village, he saw, out of the corner of his eye, John Barleycorn swaying and dancing over his grave, his long yellow beard wagging as he silently sang to the rooks in the trees.

When the others heard the news, Farmer Muck declared, "Let's get him!" and grabbed up his scythe. Farmer Mock took his sickle, and all four, armed with blades, rampaged out into the field.

*Snick-snack*, they sliced clean through him at the knees, but John Barleycorn only laughed as he fell.

*Whip-snap*, they bound him round where he lay, but John Barleycorn only laughed as they tied the knot.

*Bump-thump*, they manhandled him as far as the barn, and threw him down on the floor, where they beat him with sticks until hairs from his long beard flew amid the sunbeams. So violent and savage were they that sweat poured from their foreheads and dripped in their eyes, and their mouths were circled with a white and dusty thirst. But John Barleycorn only laughed as they pounded him.

They took his blood and bones and hid them in the water butt - and no one knew (except for the rooks in the trees) what they had done.

Then they had a feast, because John Barleycorn was dead. Mrs Mick and Mrs Mack, Mrs Mock and Mrs Muck baked loaves, and the farmers rolled the barrel from the barn all the way to the inn. The innkeeper stabbed a spike through the keg's side, and fitted a tap in the hole. And when the liquor inside glugged out into their tankards, it sounded for all the world like laughter.

"I give you a toast!" cried Farmer Mick. "John Barleycorn - may he live for ever, God bless him!" and the others took up the toast: *John Barleycorn!*

A strange thing to say, you may think, about someone you have just murdered. But not if you think first of a stalk of barley - how it grows from a seed into a green shoot; how it sways in the wind, ripens to gold in the sun and grows a whiskery beard. Reapers reap it, threshers thrash it, brewers nail it into casks. So next time Farmer Mick and Farmer Mack, Farmer Mock and Farmer Muck stagger home from the inn, their arms round each others' necks, and singing fit to frighten the rooks away, raise three hearty cheers for John Barleycorn and the barley wine that's made from him.

Well? Do you think that's water they've just been drinking?

# The Singer Above the River

A GERMAN LEGEND

A HEARTBROKEN GIRL once wandered the banks of the River Rhine. Her lover had chosen to marry someone else, and her heart was a rock within her, heavy and hard. She searched the fields for somewhere which did not remind her of her lover. She searched the woods for somewhere she could forget him. She searched the riverbank for somewhere she might sleep without dreaming of him. And when she found nowhere, she sought to end all her sorrows by dying. She threw herself from the huge black rock which juts out over the Rhine like an angry fist. Her name was Lorelei.

But even in death, Lorelei found no peace. Her soul was not permitted to rest. She was doomed, for taking her own life, to live on, in the shape of a nymph, perched on the craggy rock from which she had fallen. Her beauty was greater than it had been in life, her voice ten times more lovely. But in place of grief, she nursed a terrible hatred for young men.

As shadows appear with the sunrise, so with sunset Lorelei appeared: a wraith, a twilight shadow. Any sailor, looking up through the dusk as he sailed by, might see a white arm beckoning from the summit of the cliff. A sweet face, barely distinguishable in the half-light, would call to him, sing to him, sing such a song that he felt himself falling towards it. His hand would tug on the tiller as the voice tugged on his heart. Powerless to resist, he would steer for the crag, heel towards the grey crag and the jagged boulders which lay heaped at its feet.

As his boat split, and water closed over his head, each drowning sailor was still looking upwards, still listening to magic music. Then, as the top rim of the setting sun dipped below the horizon, Lorelei would disappear.

Word spread of the maiden on the rock - the siren who lured men to their deaths. One young man, Ronald, son of the Count Palatine, became obsessed by the thought of her. He boasted that he would lift the curse on the river. He would both remove the hazard to shipping (which was making the Rhine unnavigable) and win himself a bride in the same night. He would climb the rocks, up to the nymph called Lorelei, and snatch her from her dizzy lair. He would close her singing mouth with kisses, and rescue her damned soul by the power of true love.

In short he fell in love with the idea of Lorelei, and believed there was nothing he could not do, because that is what love does to a man.

"Ferryman, ferryman, row me past the Lorelei Rock."

"No, not for brass money, young sir, I will not."

"Ferryman, ferryman, I'll pay you silver."

"Not even silver, young sir, would make me row by the Lorelei."

"Ferryman, ferryman, then I shall pay you gold."

The ferryman hesitated. "How much gold?"

"Enough," said Ronald.

So, late in the afternoon, the ferryman settled his oars in the rowlocks, and rowed out into the current, with Ronald standing at the bow. The ferryman kept his back always to the rock so that he could not glimpse the nymph and succumb to her magic. But Ronald fixed his eyes on the

rock, and his face grew bright in the light of the setting sun.

Suddenly she appeared, the invisible taking shape, like salt settling out of sea water.

"Come," said her hands, waving. "Come," said her arms, beckoning. "Come," said her sweet red mouth, "come and take me home!"

"Row faster, ferryman," urged Ronald, "for I must climb the rock before the light fails and she disappears!"

The ferryman did not alter the steady, rhythmic dip of his oars, steering a straight course down the centre of the river.

"Faster, faster, ferryman! Look, she is ready to come with me, if I can just reach her in time!"

The ferryman said nothing, for he had seen it all happen before.

"Faster, faster, you fool!" cried Ronald, as the ferryman eased the boat carefully, carefully down the current. "You must get closer, or how can I gain a grip on the rock?"

The ferryman shipped his oars. "This is close enough, young man. You don't want to die so soon. Think what a sweet life lies ahead of you. I'll take you no farther."

"Cheat! Cheat!" raged Ronald, thinking only of the present. "I gave you gold to carry me to the rock face!"

"But what good will your gold be to me when I am dead? You have your money back, and I shall row you safe ashore."

All the while, Lorelei beckoned, whistled, sang like a calling-bird: "Come to me, love! Come and fetch me down!" In his passion to reach the singing nymph, Ronald snatched one of the oars and began to use it as a paddle. The rowing-boat rocked wildly under him and began to spin. The currents near the cliff face took hold of it and it gathered speed. Ronald gave a whoop of triumph. Too late, he realized that it was speeding towards disaster.

As the boards split between his feet and rocks came through the floor of the boat, Ronald was flung into the cold water. It held him like the arms of a woman. It covered his face with cold, wet kisses, and drew him down to join the company of other sailors wrecked on the Lorelei. The nymph high above smiled, kissed her fingertips and, leaning over the cliff edge, waved down at the drowning men, laughing.

The Count Palatine broke his chain of office between clenched fists when he was told of his son's death. "Kill that *thing* on the rock! And if it is dead already, pen its soul and torment it, slowly, for a thousand years!"

Every soldier in his service armed himself with axe or mace, pike or broadsword. The troops set sail for the Lorelei in as huge a ship as had dared to pass through the reach for many years. And when they reached the rock, it was morning and they had all day to make the climb. Studded boots scuffing the rock face, mailed gloves clinging to the fissures, they climbed, with ropes and crampons, pitons and picks. They could not hear the cry of the starlings or the redstart round their heads, for they had wax crammed in their ears to shut out the magic song of Lorelei.

Just as the first man's fingers reached over the brink of the beetling rock, the sun's bottom rim touched land. Lorelei appeared, one moment invisible, the next a woman as lovely as the trees swaying in the distant landscape.

"That's right. Come, my dear fellows. I have kisses enough for all of you! Come here, my handsome soldiers. Come home from the hardships of war to the softness of peace. Come. Come!"

But the soldiers were the cruellest and the bitterest men in all Germany - the Count had made certain of that. They had no daughters, no wives, no sweethearts. As they clambered on to the flat top of the black outcrop, Lorelei could see their ears stuffed with wax, their hands holding maces and pikes and swords.

"Despair, demon, for the Count Palatine himself has called for you to die or, if you are dead, for your soul to be penned and poked, like a pig."

"Then I call on the river!" exclaimed Lorelei, jumping to her feet and raising her voice above theirs. "You Rhine! Save your daughter Lorelei from these . . . these *beasts* disguised as men, who haven't a heart or soul between them!"

Far below, the sound of the river altered, so that the climbing soldiers looked down. They saw a wave heave itself up, as though the river itself were drawing a deep breath. The wave, as it rolled, gathered momentum, sucking water from the shore and piling it, fathom upon fathom, into a tidal wave. The wreckage of thirty ships was stirred up from the riverbed and broken anew, scattering flotsam down the flooding river.

Still the river filled, rising, rising up the sides of the gorge, until it sucked at the boots of the mountaineering soldiers. Just when they thought they had escaped its torrential spray, a second wave broke against the rock, soaking them to the skin. A third plucked men from the rock face and left them swinging on their ropes like spiders on lengths of thread. But those who had reached the top already crawled, relentless as limpets, across the wet black rock, closing in on Lorelei.

With a scream of defiance, she leapt headlong into the mountainous waves . . . and disappeared. She vanished, as surely as salt sprinkled on to water. The setting sun turned the raging river to the colour of blood before the turbulence settled, the waters fell quiet and the Rhine rolled on, black and implacable, into the coming night.

Never again did the nymph beckon from the top of the black rock, luring men to their deaths. But many were the young girls who had their hearts broken by young men, and too many were the young men who went on to become soldiers, steely in body and soul, and deaf to the sweetest singing.

# How Music was Fetched
# Out of Heaven

A MEXICAN MYTH

ONCE the world suffered in Silence. Not that it was a quiet place, nor peaceful, for there was always the groan of the wind, the crash of the sea, the grumble of lava in the throats of volcanoes, and the grate of man's ploughshare through the stony ground. Babies could be heard crying at night, and women in the daytime, because of the hardness of life and the great unfriendliness of Silence.

Tezcatlipoca, his body heavy as clay and his heart heavy as lead (for he was the Lord of Matter), spoke to Quetzalcoatl, feathery Lord of Spirit. He spoke from out of the four quarters of the Earth, from the north, south, easterly and westerly depths of the iron-hard ground. "The world needs music, Quetzalcoatl! In the thorny glades and on the bald seashore, in the square comfortless houses of the poor and in the dreams of the sleeping,

*84*

there should be music, there ought to be song. Go to Heaven, Quetzalcoatl, and fetch it down!"

"How would I get there? Heaven is higher than wings will carry me."

"String a bridge out of cables of wind, and nail it with stars: a bridge to the Sun. At the feet of the Sun, sitting on the steps of his throne, you will find four musicians. Fetch them down here. For I am so sad in this Silence, and the People are sad, hearing the sound of Nothingness ringing in their ears."

"I will do as you say," said Quetzalcoatl, preening his green feathers in readiness for the journey. "But will they come, I ask myself. Will the musicians of the Sun want to come?"

He whistled up the winds like hounds. Like hounds they came bounding over the bending treetops, over the red places where dust rose up in twisting columns, and over the sea, whipping the waters into mountainous waves. Baying and howling, they carried Quetzalcoatl higher and higher - higher than all Creation - so high that he could glimpse the Sun ahead of him. Then the four mightiest winds plaited themselves into a cable, and the cable swung out across the void of Heaven: a bridge planked with cloud and nailed with stars.

"Look out, here comes Quetzalcoatl," said the Sun, glowering, lowering, his red-rimmed eyes livid. Circling him in a cheerful dance, four musicians played and sang. One, dressed in white and shaking bells, was singing lullabies; one, dressed in red, was singing songs of war and passion as he beat on a drum; one, in sky-blue robes fleecy with cloud, sang the ballads of Heaven, the stories of the gods; one, in yellow, played on a golden flute.

This place was too hot for tears, too bright for shadows. In fact the shadows had all fled downwards and clung fast to men. And yet all this sweet music had not served to make the Sun generous. "If you don't want to have to leave here and go down where it's dark, dank, dreary and dangerous, keep silent, my dears. Keep silent, keep secret, and don't answer when Quetzalcoatl calls," he warned his musicians.

Across the bridge rang Quetzalcoatl's voice. "O singers! O marvellous makers of music. Come to me. The Lord of the World is calling!" The voice

of Quetzalcoatl was masterful and inviting, but the Sun had made the musicians afraid. They kept silent, crouching low, pretending not to hear. Again and again Quetzalcoatl called them, but still they did not stir, and the Sun smiled smugly and thrummed his fingers on the sunny spokes of his chairback. He did not intend to give up his musicians, no matter who needed them.

So Quetzalcoatl withdrew to the rain-fringed horizon and, harnessing his four winds to the black thunder, had them drag the clouds closer, circling the Sun's citadel. When he triggered the lightning and loosed the thunderclaps, the noise was monumental. The Sun thought he was under siege.

Thunder clashed against the Sun with the noise of a great brass cymbal, and the musicians, their hands over their ears, ran this way and that looking for help. "Come out to me, little makers of miracles," said Quetzalcoatl in a loud but gentle voice. *BANG* went the thunder, and all Heaven shook.

The crooner of lullabies fluttered down like a sheet blown from a bed. The singer of battle-songs spilled himself like blood along the floor of Heaven and covered his head with his arms. The singer of ballads, in his fright, quite forgot his histories of Heaven, and the flautist dropped his golden flute. Quetzalcoatl caught it.

As the musicians leapt from their fiery nest, he opened his arms and welcomed them into his embrace, stroking their heads in his lap. "Save us, Lord of Creation! The Sun is under siege!"

"Come, dear friends. Come where you are needed most."

The Sun shook and trembled with rage like a struck gong, but he knew he had been defeated, had lost his musicians to Quetzalcoatl.

At first the musicians were dismayed by the sadness and silence of the Earth. But no sooner did they begin to play than the babies in their cribs stopped squalling. Pregnant women laid a hand on their big stomachs and sighed with contentment. The man labouring in the field cupped a hand to his ear and shook himself, so that his shadow of sadness fell away in the noonday. Children started to hum. Young men and women got up to dance, and in dancing fell in love. Even the mourner at the graveside, hearing sweet flute music, stopped crying.

Quetzalcoatl himself swayed his snaky hips and lifted his hands in dance at the gate of Tezcatlipoca, and Tezcatlipoca came out of doors. Matter and Spirit whirled together in a dance so fast: had you been there, you would have thought you were seeing only one.

And suddenly every bird in the sky opened its beak and sang, and the stream moved by with a musical ripple. The sleeping child dreamed music and woke up singing. From that day onwards, life was all music - rhythms and refrains, falling cadences and fluting calls. No one saw just where the Sun's musicians settled or made their homes, but their footprints were everywhere and their bright colours were found in corners that had previously been grey and cobwebbed with silence. The flowers turned up bright faces of red and yellow and white and blue, as if they could hear singing. Even the winds ceased to howl and roar and groan, and learned love songs.

# Whose Footprints?

## A MYTH FROM THE GOLD COAST

DO YOU SUPPOSE God made the world all by himself? Of course not. He had help. He had a servant. Every Fon in Abomey knows that. The servant's name was Legba, and he took the blame for whatever went wrong.

Whenever the people saw a wonderful sunset, or made a huge catch of fish, they gave thanks to God and said, "Great is our Creator, who has made all things wonderfully well!"

Whenever they fell over a rock, or the canoe sank, they said, "Legba is making mischief again. That villain Legba!"

Now Legba thought this was mortally unfair. "Why do I get all the blame?" he complained.

"That's what you're there for," said God. "It wouldn't do for people to think of God as anything but perfect. It would set them a bad example."

"But they hate me!" protested Legba. "They hang up charms at their doors to keep me out, and they frighten their children with my name: 'Be good or Legba will come and steal you out of your bed!' How would you feel?" But God had already sauntered away towards the garden where he grew yams. (This was in the days when God lived on Earth, among all that he had made.)

God tended those yams with loving care and attention. If the truth were told, he was kept so busy by his gardening some days, that things could go wrong in the world without him really noticing. It did not matter. Legba got the blame, naturally.

Legba sat down and thought. Then Legba stood up and spoke. "Lord, I hear that thieves are planning to steal your yams tonight!"

God was horrified. He sounded a ram's-horn trumpet and summoned together all the people of the world. They came, jostling and bowing, smiling and offering presents. They were rather taken aback to see God so angry.

"If any one of you intends to rob my garden tonight, I'm telling you here and I'm telling you now, and I'm making it plain as day: that thief shall die!"

The people clutched each other and trembled. They nodded feverishly to show they had understood, hurried home to their beds and pulled the covers over their heads until morning. God watched them scatter and brushed together the palms of his great hands. "That settles that," he said, and went home to bed himself.

Legba waited. When all sound had ceased but the scuttle of night creatures, the flutter of bats and the drone of snoring humanity, he crept into God's house. God, too, was snoring. Legba wormed his way across the floor, and stole the sandals from beside God's bed.

Putting on the sandals, he crept to the yam garden. Though the shoes were over-large and tripped him more than once, he worked his way from tree to tree, removing every delectable yam. The dew glistened, the ground was wet. The sandals of God left deep prints in the moist soil . . .

"Come quick! Come quick! The thief has struck!"

God tumbled out of bed, fumbled his feet into his sandals and stumbled out of doors into the first light of morning. When he saw the waste that had been laid to his garden, the shout could be heard all the way to Togo.

"Don't worry! Don't worry!" Legba hurried to console him. "Look how the thief has left his footprints in the ground! You have only to find the

shoes that made those footprints, and you will have caught the culprit red-handed . . . -footed, I mean."

Once more, the ram's-horn sounded, and the people pelted out of their huts and horded into God's presence, trembling.

"*Someone* has stolen my yams!" bellowed God. "*Someone* is about to *DIE*!"

They all had to fetch out their sandals, and every sandal was laid against the footprints in the garden. But not one fitted. Not one.

"Legba! Try Legba! He's always doing wicked things!" shouted the people, and Legba felt that familiar pang of resentment that God did not correct them. It would have been nice if God could have said, "Oh not *Legba*. He's entirely trustworthy. He helped me create the world. He's my good and faithful servant." Not a bit of it.

"*Legba! Have you been stealing from me?!*"

Willingly Legba produced his sandals. Willingly he laid them alongside the footprints in the garden. But not by any stretch of the imagination did Legba's sandals fit the prints beneath the yam trees.

"Perhaps you walked in your sleep, O Lord?" suggested Legba, and the people all said, "AAAH!"

God tried to look disdainful of such a ridiculous suggestion, but the eyes of all Creation were gazing at him, waiting. He laid his great foot alongside one of the great footprints, and the people gasped and laughed and sighed with relief. It was just God, walking in his sleep, ha ha ha! God was to blame after all!

Then they began to wonder - God could see the question form in their faces - if God had sleepwalked once, perhaps he had sleepwalked before. And if God stole in his sleep, what else might he get up to under the cover of darkness, under the influence of his dreams?

God glowered at Legba. He knew Legba had something to do with his embarrassment, but could not quite see what. Instead, he stamped his sandalled foot irritably and said, "I'm going! I'm not staying here where no one gives me the respect I deserve! I'm going *higher up*!"

So God moved higher up. And he told Legba to report to him every night, in the sky, with news of what people were getting up to.

Of course what Legba chooses to tell God is entirely up to Legba. But the Fon of Abomey have been a lot nicer to Legba since God went higher up. A lot nicer.

# The Death of El Cid

A SPANISH LEGEND

DON RODRIGO DÍAZ DE VIVAR was cursed with pride. It was pride which caused his banishment from the court of King Alfonso of Spain. It was pride which made him swear never to cut his beard until his banishment was repealed. It was pride which made him venture out from Alfonso's tiny corner-kingdom into the part of Spain that had been occupied by Moors from North Africa, where it was certain death for any Christian to go.

Into Moorish Spain he charged, first with a dozen men, then with a hundred, then with a thousand at his back. Before him fell village after fortress, city after port. And from every victory he sent the spoils back to King Alfonso, his King, his lord and master, to whom his obedience never faltered. Still the King did not pardon him, but many more young men left

94

Alfonso's kingdom to join Rodrigo de Vivar and find their fortunes in conquest.

The Moorish occupiers were swept away like rabbits before a heath fire. Families who had lived for generations in Spain, and thought themselves its owners, fled to Africa or had to buy back their lives and freedom from Rodrigo de Vivar. They called him, in their own tongue, El Siddi - the War Lord - and his own men took it up: *"El Cid! Viva El Cid!"* He captured Moorish towns like so many pieces in a game of chess.

At last only one black piece was left standing on the board of Spain: Valencia, the treasure-house of the Moors. Not till then did the African might of Islam stir itself. Valencia must not be allowed to fall, or all Spain would be in the hands of Christians.

Before the fleets of Africa could touch Spanish shores, Valencia had fallen, and El Cid, the victor, had made the exquisite city his own. Sending for his wife and family, he celebrated the marriage of his two daughters, and glorified in the King's forgiveness. His joy was complete. He decided to live out his days in Valencia, for there is nowhere lovelier under God's gaze.

On the night of the double wedding, a little, cowardly, creeping man crawled through the flowery grass on his belly, with a heart full of envy. He pushed a knife through the cloth of a tent, and stabbed El Cid in the back, sinking his blade up to the haft.

Within days, the Moorish legions landed in thousands and tens of thousands, and laid siege to the city - pitched their tents among the orange groves and awaited with impatience the day Valencia's citizens would thirst and starve to death.

"But we have El Cid!" cried the people in the streets. "With El Cid to lead us, we have nothing to fear!" And they jeered over the walls at the besieging army. "El Cid will crop you like oranges!"

But El Cid lay bleeding on his bed, his life ebbing away. Nothing but a miracle would put him back astride his horse at the head of an army. When word spread of Don Rodrigo's injury, terror and despair poisoned the streets like acrid smoke.

"El Cid is dying!"

"El Cid is at death's door!"

"El Cid is dead!"

No word came from the window of his house. No news, either good or bad, came from the lips of El Cid's wife, the lovely Jimena. She sat beside her husband's bed, her long hair spread on the coverlet, and her eyes resting on the distant sea. When at last she opened the door, it was to say, "Fetch El Cid's horse to the door and you, Alvar Fanez, come and help Don Rodrigo to put on his armour."

Alvar was El Cid's closest friend, his most trusted servant. He ran into the room in a fervour of delight. The saints had restored his master's health! El Cid was fit to lead his army into battle!

Alvar Fanez fell back, his mouth open to speak, his heart half broken by what he saw. The craggy features of Don Rodrigo de Vivar lay whiter than the pillow, his eyes were shut, his hands lay crossed on his breast.

"He's dead," was all he could think of to say.

"Yes," said Jimena, simply and calmly, "but his name will live for ever, and it is his name which must save the city today. Help me arm my husband one last time, and tie him on to his horse. I believe that El Cid can still carry the day, if only he shows himself on the battlefield."

Alvar Fanez did as he was asked. Together - though it was a terrible ordeal for the two alone - they tied Don Rodrigo to his horse for one last ride. Jimena kissed her husband farewell. Alvar Fanez mounted, and led the general's horse to the city gate.

Ahead went the incredulous whispers, the gasps of happy amazement in the half-light of morning.

"El Cid is alive!"

"He's going to head the attack!"

Silently, so as to surprise the sleeping Moors, the army mustered in the streets behind the gate. Division upon division formed rank. As dawn broke, the knights of El Cid struggled to hold their horses in check between the shadowy houses of Valencia.

At the crash of the crossbar unfastening the gate, El Cid's horse Babeica pawed the ground. It leapt past Alvar Fanez in the open gateway and lunged into the lead, as it had in a hundred battles.

The Moors, waking to the sound of galloping horses, looked out of their tent flaps to see the hosts of El Cid riding down on them. The knights of Islam called for their armour. Their squires ran to and fro with weapons and bridles. "To arms! To arms!"

"Huh!" sneered King Mu'taman of Morocco, walking with showy disdain to the stirrup of his mount. "My assassin has cut the heart out of El Cid. My spies have confirmed it. And what is an army without its heart?"

Then he saw a sight which struck such horror into him that his foot missed the stirrup and his shaking legs would not hold him. He fell to his knees, calling on the one true god of Islam for help. "Can the man not die? Is this why he brought our empires to nothing? Is he immortal? Is it a ghost we have to fight now?" For riding towards him - directly towards him - was the tall, erect, unmistakable figure of El Cid, conqueror of Spain,

in full panoply of armour but bareheaded, his long grey hair and beard streaming.

The King's trembling fingers searched for his lance, and he threw it at the chest of El Cid. But though it struck home, the conqueror did not flinch. It was his horse's hooves which trampled the King of Morocco and which tumbled his tasselled tent to the ground. El Cid rode on, so appalling the superstitious enemy that they flung themselves into the sea sooner than face a ghostly enemy who would not, could not die.

Out of the orange groves and along the beaches of Valencia rode Don Rodrigo de Vivar, on his last foray. From the city walls, Dona Jimena watched till he was no longer in sight. But she shed no tears. She knew it was not the ghost of El Cid out there; it was his flesh, his blood. But neither was it El Cid himself. She knew that the soul of El Cid was at rest, and that his spirit was ranging free, untethered and invisible, high above the heads of his victorious army.

# The Man Who Almost Lived for Ever

A MESOPOTAMIAN LEGEND

LONG AGO, when the history of Humankind could still be carved on a single pillar, there lived two friends. One, Adapa the Priest, was the wisest of men. The other, Ea, was the friendliest of the gods. But you would have thought they were brothers. Ea taught Adapa many things never before known by mortals - how to speak magic, for instance, and carry it in the fingers of his hand.

Adapa was fishing alone one day, in a stretch of water where the river Euphrates widens into a gleaming lake. A storm sprang up and spilled him out of his boat, wetting his venerable beard and his priestly robes and his dignity. Adapa swam to the shore and pulled himself out, dripping wet. Then he pointed a finger at the South Wind and pronounced a curse, as Ea had taught him to do.

"Come down on you the very worst;
May every power of yours be burst.
You have a mighty wrath incurred,
Therefore be broken, like a bird.
Oh vile South Wind, I call you CURSED!"

Like a great albatross shot from the sky, the South Wind drooped and
faltered. One wing was snapped by Adapa's piercing curse, and the wind
limped to its nest with an eerie, lamenting cry, and left the banners of
seventy kings drooping. The gods in Heaven were shocked.

"Who taught this small worthless man of the Earth the magic words of
Heaven? Ea? Why have you shared our secrets with this puny mortal?
Summon him before us, to explain himself!"

Ea told Adapa of the summons. "Don't worry, friend. You have wisdom
enough to speak well, and I will commend you to the gods. Tammuz and
Gizidu will meet you at the gates, and conduct you before the throne of
Mighty Anu. I have asked them, too, to speak well of you in the Courts of
Heaven . . . Just one word of advice." Adapa, who had already begun to
rehearse what he would say to the gods, looked round at the change in
Ea's voice. "Be on your guard, Adapa. The gods are cunning, and you have
angered them. They may offer you bread and oil to eat. On no account
accept it. It may be poisoned."

Meanwhile, the gods discussed among themselves what was to be done
about Adapa and his great knowledge.

"We could strike him dead," said one.

"We could just tell him never to use magic again," said another.

"We could always make him immortal, like us," said a third.

"Or there again . . ."

Shortly, Tammuz and Gizidu led Adapa in front of Anu's throne.

"Adapa, you are accused of cursing the South Wind and of breaking its
white wing with the magic words of the gods. Is this true?"

"I admit it," said Adapa. "The South Wind wrecked me and endangered
my life." The gods listened. Some nodded, some glared, some leaned their

heads together in debate. Adapa began to feel more confident. "As for the curse I used, I was taught it by my good friend Ea, who has introduced me to many such marvels."

"Before I give judgement," said Anu suddenly, "you must take some refreshment. You've had a long journey. Tammuz! Bring bread and oil!"

It was a gracious offer, courteously made, but Adapa flinched. Tammuz lifted a tray from a table: a flagon of oil and a broken loaf of hot sweet-smelling bread.

Though Adapa was very hungry, he held up a regal hand.

"With your indulgence, I won't eat. I've had enough already. I rarely take more than one meal a day."

To Adapa's alarm, the Mighty Anu suddenly fell back in his throne and slapped his knees. "You see? You see!" he bellowed at the other, lesser gods. "You see how stupid these little Earthmen are? Adapa, you're a fool, for all your wisdom! I said you weren't worthy! I said you wouldn't know what to do with it! But I never thought you'd turn it down! Ha ha ha! Turned it down! No immortal would have been so stupid! Go back to your temples and your prayers. Go back to your *little* life full of *little* achievements. Go back with your talk of visiting Heaven: no one will believe you. Go home now, Adapa, for we offered you the bread and oil of everlasting life, and you turned it down. So *die*!"

Adapa ran all the way back down to Earth. For the rest of his short life, he went over and over that day in his head - and how he had come to make his worst of all mistakes. Had the gods tricked him? Or had Ea? It was Ea who had told him not to eat. Had Ea given his advice in good faith?

Ea and Adapa no longer fished together in the lakes of the Euphrates, because Adapa could never be sure. Once such doubts have entered a friendship, the friendship has already begun to crumble. Ea and Adapa fished together no more, and one day, when the South Wind had recovered its strength, it spilled Adapa into deeper water, where he drowned.

He was only mortal, after all.

# Stealing Heaven's Thunder

A NORSE MYTH

IN THE HIGH halls of Valhalla, across the Rainbow Bridge, in the realm called Asgard, Thor the God of Thunder woke. He lay for a while between the damp softnesses of dark cloud, and contemplated the day ahead.

"Today," he said, "I shall reshape the mountains with my hammer, smash the ice cap to the north into glassy spinters, and make the valleys boom like cannon fire. I'll strike lightning from the anvil Earth and shoe Odin's horse with gold from the mines of Middle Earth!" He rolled out of bed, clutched about him a robe of black fur, and reached for his blacksmith's hammer.

It was not in its usual place.

He searched under the bed and in every cavernous cupboard of his chamber. He searched the stairways and corridors of Valhalla, in every trunk and chest, on every landing, in the smithy and the treasury, his temper growing with the increasing daylight.

"*WHERE'S MY HAMMER?*" he bellowed at last, and Valhalla shook.

Other gods joined in the search. Queen Freya herself, wrapped in her flying cloak, soared among the pinnacles of Heaven, thinking to glimpse the hammer from the air. Then Odin, King of the Gods, banged a door or two, and scowled.

"It's plain that Thor's hammer has been stolen. Who would - who could - steal such a prize, but those grunting grubs, the Giants?"

"Take my cloak, Loki," said the Queen, "and go quickly to the Realm of Giants. Find out if it is true."

Loki sped across the Rainbow Bridge, down through the ether, and, tumbling like a pigeon, landed at the gate of the Giants' castle.

"It's true we have Thor's hammer," bragged the largest of the castle's warriors, Din. "It's true, too, that you will never find where it's hidden. For I've buried the great hammer called Thunderbolt under clods of clay, one

mile underground, and the place is known only to me." Din scratched his tunic of mangey bear fur, and a cloud of dust enveloped them both. He sneezed, wiped his nose on a mat of greasy hair, and leered at Loki. "I want a bride, see. And that's my bride-price: Thor's hammer in exchange for a wife!"

Loki was almost relieved. "I'm certain that somewhere in the world Odin can find you a suitable . . ."

"Oh, I *know* he can," Din interrupted, cleaning out his ears with a piece of stick, "and he won't have to look far to find her. I mean to marry Freya. Just for once, what's good enough for the gods might be good enough for me. Now you go and tell Odin: no Freya, no Thunderbolt! And let him send her soon - within three days! I'm weary of being a bachelor." Loki turned in disgust to go. "Oh, and say she must bring that flying cloak of hers! And her magic golden necklace!" Din laughed till his nose ran and, blowing his nose between finger and thumb, flapped his hands together with all the grace of an elephant seal.

On the return flight, Loki considered the filthy bargain. Odin would never agree to giving away his wife. He would declare war at the very suggestion. But, in the meantime, what damage would the Giants do to Middle Earth with Thor's hammer? They would flatten its crags, terrorize its occupants. The little humans would blame the gods for their persecution, and the foundations of Valhalla would shake at the consequences. By the time he crossed the Rainbow Bridge of Asgard, Loki had formulated his own solution to the problem.

"Lord Odin, King of Gods and mightiest of us all, I bring word from the thieves who stole Thor's hammer. They have placed a price on its return . . ."

Three days later, bride and escort set out from Valhalla, canopied beneath Queen Freya's cobalt-blue cloak.

Seeing the two figures descend out of the sunshine, Din clapped his hands once more. "Prepare a feast! Come, brother Giants, and be my guests! Today is my wedding day!" The worm-eaten table in the Castle of Giants groaned under the weight of food. Barrels of wine were stacked as high as the bat-infested vaults of the roof, and a place of honour was cleared among the litter for the bench of bride and groom.

First Loki entered, then the bride, veiled and shining behind him. "I bring Freya, formerly Queen of Heaven," announced Loki grandly, "to be Queen among Giants and wife to Din!"

Din looked on with a fixed grin of sheepish delight, as the bride seated herself and lifted her veil to eat. Two golden plaits as long as bell ropes coiled themselves on the floor to either side of her. She leaned forward and took a rack of lamb, reducing it to a pile of bones in moments. Next she ate a side of beef and three brace of partridge. Then, impatient of the servingman's slowness in filling her glass, she took the jug from him and emptied it in a single swig.

"You certainly do enjoy your food," giggled Din admiringly. "A woman after my own heart. But how do you keep your figure?"

Loki, seated on Din's other side, caught him by the sleeve and whispered confidentially, "She's been so agitated at the thought of meeting you, my lord Din, that she hasn't eaten for three days. She's making up for lost time, that's all."

Din scratched his neck with a hambone. "Agitated, eh? Is that good or bad?" he whispered back.

"Oh, my dear fellow!" Loki had his head almost inside the Giant's gigantic ear, so as not to be overheard. "I think she must have nursed a passion for you this many a year! You've never seen a woman in such a fever to get to her wedding, I do assure you! That Odin - he may be handsome, clever, noble, brave, powerful . . . but he's not every woman's idea of the ideal lover, you know?"

Din turned crimson with delight, and exhaled a sigh with breath like rotting cabbage leaves. "She loves me?" Turning to his bride, he said, "Well, don't be shy, then: kiss me, woman!"

Blue eyes looked back at him, as wild as the sea, then changed to the colour of ice, before darkening to scarlet. They blazed in their sockets, those eyes.

Din gulped and shuffled back along the bench, edging Loki on to the floor without noticing. "Why's she look at me like that?"

"Passion," replied Loki succinctly. "Now, there's just the matter of Thor's hammer . . ."

He had almost reached his feet again when Din clapped him violently on the back and sent him sprawling. "Of course! I'm a man of my bond! Thor's hammer for a bride, I said, and that's what I meant." A nod of his great head sent a dozen servants running, spades in hand, to unearth the hammer called Thunderbolt. When they returned with it, Din had just plucked up the courage to tickle the back of Freya's neck with his big fingers.

The servants grunted and staggered under the hammer's great weight, and the table collapsed as they set it down. But nothing could dent Din's

pleasure. "I'd like to see Odin's face when he finds out his beloved Freya's left him for a giant like me!"

For the first time, the bride spoke. "Then you shall have your wish, Din!"

Pulling off her plaits, the bride snatched up the stolen hammer and whirled it round, before letting it fall on the top of Din's verminous head. Freed of his disguise at last, Odin smashed the tuns of red wine, brought down the vaulted roof. He knocked giants as far as the northern sea and the Baltic Straits. He frightened off their giant cows and stampeded their giant horses, and left their armoury a tangle of twisted metal in the bottom of a fjord.

Only the thin air of Asgard could cool his blazing temper, and he berated Loki continually on the flight back for thinking up such a plan. "A giant paddling his fingers in my neck, indeed! A giant trying to kiss me!"

Queen Freya saw them rising, like gulls on a warm wind, and greeted her husband's return with pleasure, though she had no idea where he had been.

"Why ever are you wearing that dress, Odin?" she asked. "It doesn't suit you at all . . . But I'm glad to see you've brought Thor's hammer back. He's been wretched without it."

Reunited with his Thunderbolt, Thor, God of Thunder, raced around Heaven, striking sparks from the crags of Norway, fires from the peaks of Iceland. He bruised the clouds to a blackness, then split them and loosed a cascade of rain on the fires he had just lit with lightning. Never was there such a storm as the night Thor got back his hammer.

But within the high halls of Valhalla, Freya and Odin slept through the storm undisturbed, while Loki, alone and unthanked, brooded on the idea of making more mischief . . .

# Anansi and the Mind of God

A WEST INDIAN MYTH

ANANSI was an African. Spider-man Anansi. But he stowed away on a slave ship to the West Indies, so now he turns up in Jamaica and suchlike, as sneaky as a tarantula in a hand of bananas. Spider-man Anansi, Anansi the Trickster. They do say Anansi's the cleverest creature next to God . . . or was it Anansi said that?

Now Spider-man Anansi was a clever man,
But he got to boasting he was God's right hand.
Said God, "Anansi, if you're really so smart,
You can tell what I'm thinking in my heart of hearts.
There's three things I want, and if you're my peer,
You'll have no trouble in fetching them here."

Well, Spider-man Anansi, he up and fled,
Swinging down from Heaven on his long black thread.
He ain't one clue what he's s'pose' to fetch back,
But he ain't gonna let God Almighty know that.
He seeks out the birdies, one, two, three;
Says, "Spare one feather for Mister Anansi!"
Asks every bird for just one feather,
Then Anansi-man, he sews them together.

He sews him a glorious rainbow suit:
Feather pyjamas, feather mask and boots,
Then off he flies high up in the sky,
And he dances about till he takes God's eye.
God says, "Well Lordy, and upon my word!
Who's gonna tell me 'bout this rainbow bird?
I know I didn't make it, so who else did?"
And he asked the mack'rel and he asked the squid.
He asked the turtle and he asked the dog,
And he asked the monkey and he asked the frog,
And he asked the bird, but it just jumped by,
Giving out a perfume like a rainbow pie.

Now God's advisors racked their brains all day,
But they couldn't find but one thing to say:
"Anansi's the man who could solve this case."
Says God, "But I sent *him* on a wild-goose chase!
I sent him to fetch three things to me:
So I fear that's the end of old Anansi."
"Why? What did you send him for, Lord?" ask they.
"For the night and the moon and the light of day.
Not that I said so. No, I made him guess,
'Cos he got to boasting he was better than best.
But now he's gone, well, I'm sorry, kinda -

That I told Anansi to be a read-minder."
All the creatures laughed, but God wasn't luffin',
When away flew the bird like a shaggy puffin.

It was no sooner gone than who comes in,
But Spider Anansi in his own black skin.
In came Anansi with a bulging sack.
Says, "Sorry I kept you, Lord, but now I'm back.
Anansi-man's back and I think you'll find
I've brought you the three things were on your mind."
So he reaches in the sack and oh! what a fright,
He plunges Heaven into darkest night.
Out comes the moon next with a silv'ry shine
And God says, "Mercy me, I thought I'd gone blind!
Touché, Anansi-man, you got me licked.
I don't know how, but I know I been tricked."
Then Anansi pulls out the great big sun -
All its terrible bright illu-min-a-tion,
And it burns God's eyeball in a place or two,
And it gives him pain, and it spoils his view.

So when God looks down now from his throne on high,
There's a patch he misses with his sun-scorched eye.
You can bet that Spider-man knows where it be -
That patch of ground God Almighty can't see.

Is that where you're hiding, Mister Anansi?

# How Men and Women Finally Agreed

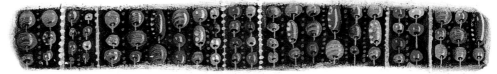

HAVING CREATED all the beauties of Africa, the Creator of course chose the most lovely for his home - the Mountain of Bright Mystery. There he lived invisible, like a patch of sunlight travelling over the mountainside, and from there he could see all over the world.

To his three sons, he offered three gifts: a hoe, a spear, a bow and arrow.

Masai, a fierce boy who loved a fight, chose the spear.

"Then you shall be a cowherd and live on the plains where the grazing is sweet," said the Creator to Masai.

Kamba, who loved to eat meat, chose the bow and arrow.

"You shall be a hunter in the forests where the wild beasts have their lairs," said the Creator to Kamba.

Kikuyu, a gentle, industrious boy, chose the hoe - which pleased his father greatly. After the others had left, the Creator kept Kikuyu by him and taught him all the secrets of agriculture - where to sow, when to reap, how to graft and propagate, which insects to encourage and which to drive away. He led Kikuyu to the top of the Bright Mountain and pointed far off.

"You see there - in the centre of the world - where those fig trees stand like a crowd of whisperers? Make your home there, my son, and may your life and the lives of your children be happy."

The figs were large and juicy, the shade deep and dark. But those were not the best things about the grove of fig trees at the centre of the world. When he got there, Kikuyu found awaiting him a beautiful wife - Moombi - and nine lovely daughters, each as dark and sweet as a fig.

For a long time, Kikuyu lived happily, planting a garden in the shade of the fig trees, as well as fields round about. His daughters helped him, singing while they worked, and the sound of Moombi's laughter rang out from time to time as she pounded maize with her pestle.

But as he watched the bees fumbling the flowers, heard the birds sing in courtship, saw the sheep lambing in the long grass, Kikuyu could not help but wonder how his daughters would ever marry and have children to make them laugh as Moombi laughed. One day, the whole family left the grove of fig trees and trekked back across the plain, past the forests and back to the Bright Mountain, to ask the Creator's advice.

"I would like the sound of men's voices in my fields and, to tell true, my nine daughters would greatly like the sight of men's faces coming home from the fields at night," Kikuyu confided in his father. "What should I do to have sons-in-law?"

"Go home, Kikuyu. Go home. And remember - the name of Kikuyu is precious to me, but the name of Moombi is sacred."

Too gentle to press his request any further, Kikuyu did as he was told, and the family trooped back, past the forest and over the plain, to the fig-tree grove.

There, leaning on their hoes, stood nine fine young men, a little startled to find themselves so suddenly called into being by the Creator. When they saw Kikuyu's nine daughters, their faces broke into the broadest of grins.

"Oh, Papa!" cried the girls, behind him. "Aren't they *lovely!*"

Kikuyu considered the words of the Creator. "Is marriage agreeable to you?" he asked the young men.

"Yes, sir!"

"And is marriage agreeable to you, daughters?"

"Oh *yes*, Papa!"

"And is it to your liking, Moombi, that our daughters marry these young men?"

"High time, and none too soon!" declared Moombi, laughing loudly.

"Then I have only this to say," announced Kikuyu. "My daughters may marry you, young men . . ."

"Oh, thank you!"

"... provided you take the name of Moombi for your family name and obey your wives in all things."

The young men made no objection, and their marriages were long and happy. When, after many years, a couple died, their hut and hoe and inheritance passed to any daughters they might have, not to the sons. The daughters chose whom they wished to marry - taking two or three or ten husbands if they wished, and that is how the family of Kikuyu and Moombi grew into a tribe.

After many generations, the men grew restive. One was jealous of his wife's other husbands. One objected to doing all the washing. One resented bitterly that his wife beat him when the sheep got loose in the garden. One felt sorry for his sons, that they would never inherit a thing. So the men muttered mutinously together, deep in the fig-tree groves, and plotted to end their wives' supremacy. But what could they do? The women fought better, ran faster, cursed louder and thought quicker than their menfolk.

So the men waited their chance. They waited until the women were all expecting babies. They waited till their wives were all half as big as hippopotami and waddling like ducks.

"*We* want to be in charge now," the men announced one day, and all the women could do was press their hands to the smalls of their backs and groan.

After that, the men took as many wives as they wanted: two or ten or twenty, and some beat their wives when the sheep got loose in the garden, and some put their wives to washing and cooking all day. When they held council, only men were invited, and, of course, they passed laws in favour of men.

"Wives!" they said one day. "We have decided we no longer want our children to carry your female family names. Our families shall have male names from now on. And no longer will the tribe be called the Moombi Kikuyu, after a woman, but rather the . . ."

"*Enough!*" A sun-wrinkled mother, big as a wildebeest and quite as handsome, stood up. She drew her brightly dyed robes around her big

baby-filled belly and settled the scarlet cloths on her head. "In that case we will bear you no more sons," she said. "The name of Kikuyu is precious in the ear of God, but the name of Moombi is sacred. If you do this thing, we who are pregnant shall give birth only to daughters; afterwards we shall bear no children at all! If you want sons, from now on, give birth to them *yourselves*!"

The other women began to laugh and nod. The men looked down at their own thin waists and narrow hips and considered the possibility. Have children? No. That was one privilege the women were welcome to.

"What are we called?" asked the wildebeest woman.

"Moombi! Moombi!" answered the women and began to chant the sacred name of the first wife: *"Moombi! Moombi! Moombi!"*

"What are we called?"

*"Moombi! Moombi! Moombi!"*

The men bowed their heads and shuffled their feet in the dust.

"How are we called?"

*"By the name of our mothers! Moombi! Moombi! Moombi!"*

"Who was our first mother?"

*"Moombi! Moombi! Moombi!"*

"What shall we call our daughters?"

*"Moombi! Moombi! Moombi!"*

"And what shall we call our sons?"

The men drummed their hoes against the ground, joined in the chanting, and consoled themselves that it was a small concession to make. They were still the ones in charge. Really.

*"Moombi! Moombi! Moombi!"*

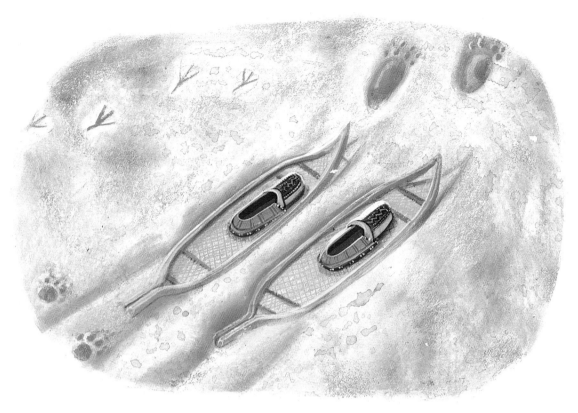

# First Snow

THE WORLD was complete.

"And yet it could be better still," said First Man, gazing up at the night sky. So he and First Woman and Coyote searched about for something to make midnight still more beautiful: a single golden stone to embed in the northern sky, three glowing red pebbles, and a handful of glittering dust which whirled and whorled in a wild, disordered dance.

"I believe we have finished," said First Man. "Life is still hard for the People, with famine and thirst in between the rains, but it is better than before, when we lived below, in the kernel of the world."

"I have one present more to give them," said Coyote.

Next morning, the People woke to see a brightness brighter than sunshine in the doors of their hogans.

They ran outside, and saw a strange and beautiful white powder falling from the sky. The first snow ever to fall on the world was whitening the bluffs, pillowing the ground, and settling in glittering swags on the trees. Flakes hung on the warp and weft of the weaving looms, like blossom on a spider's web.

The People stood stock-still, their hands outstretched, catching the snow on their palms. It was not cold. First Woman blinked the snowflakes off her eyelashes and shook them from her hair. She took a spoon and lifted a mouthful of snow to her lips.

It was delicious.

The people licked their snowy fingers.

It was delectable.

Soon everyone was scooping up the fallen snow, cramming it into their mouths. It tasted rather like buffalo dripping. They caught the falling snow in baskets, stuffed it into skin bags and stored it up in jars. They filled their pockets and piled it on the papooses. The women carried the white stuff back to their hogans in their skirts, and kneaded it into wafer bread.

"At last we shan't be hungry any more!" they sang. "Now everything is perfect!" And they feasted greedily on the magic sky food, until they grew too thirsty to eat any more.

Coyote had filled a cooking pot with white handfuls from a drift of snow. He lit a fire and smoke curled up into the sky, fraying it to grey. He began to cook the snow. The People crowded round to see what delicious stew he was making. But as they watched, they began to shiver.

First the snow in the pot turned grey, then to transparent liquid, seething, bubbling, boiling and steaming, cooling only as the fire burned out. As it did so, the snow on the trees wept and dripped and dropped down in icy tears. The white on the ground changed to a grey slush that soaked the children's moccasins, and the women let fall their skirtfuls of snow, crying, "Oh! Urgh! So cold! So wet! Urgh! Oh!" The old people drew their shawls about their heads and shook their wet mittens, disconsolate.

"Now look what you've done!" cried First Woman, wrapping herself

tight in a dozen shawls. "Our lovely food has rotted away and there's nothing left but the juices. What a wicked waste! You always were a trouble-maker, Coyote! In the time before the world, you were always making mischief, stealing, tricking, complaining. But this is the worst! You've made all our beautiful sky flour melt away!"

The People tried to pelt him with snowballs, but the snow only turned to water in their palms.

Coyote simply drank from the pot of melted snow, then shook his head so hard that his yellow ears rattled.

"You don't understand," he said gently. "Snow was not meant for food. It was sent down upon the five mountaintops for the springtime sun to melt, drip joining drop, dribble joining trickle, stream joining river, filling the lakes and pools and ponds, before it rolls down to the sea. Now, when you are thirsty, you need not wait for the rain, or catch the raindrops in your hands. You can drink whenever you please.

"The snowmelt rivers will water the woods and swell the berries for you to pick. The streams will turn the desert into grass-green grazing, so that your sheep put on wool like fleecy snow. And out there, on the plains, the bison will wade knee-deep in seas of waving grass, and grow into fat and shining herds.

"The dusty hunter can wash the sweat from his face where the young women's long wet hair streams out like weed. The children can leap and swim beside waterfalls where the poet makes verses.

"And at the end of the day, if you are still, and patient and quiet, the deer may come down to drink, and the swallows sip flies off the surface of the stream. The women weavers can wash their wools, and dye them brighter colours of the autumn woods.

"And when the summer dust settles and the ants swarm around the food baskets, and the flies buzz after the dirt, we shall wash our homes clean and sluice the summer sickness out of doors.

"Quick! There will be fish coming down the rivers - gold and silver and speckled like brown eggs. Make fishing rods and nets! Catch and bake the fish over your fires! They will taste better than any snow.

"And when First Snow falls out there in the canyons and winding places, you huntsmen will be able to find the tracks of the woolly bison with barely a glance. The footprints of the secret hare will be as plain to read on the ground, as the stars are in the sky.

"These are the uses of snow."

"So *that* was the present you had to give us, Coyote!" said First Woman, smiling.

"Oh!" yelped Coyote. "No! The snow almost made me forget!"

He ran to his hogan and fetched out several bags which he opened and spilled on the ground. There was seed inside - maize and beans and squash - and these were his present to the People. They planted gardens, and the snowmelt watered the soil, so that their gardens grew into magic larders of food far more delicious and nutritious than snow.

So next year, when the First Snow fell, the People held a great feast to celebrate its coming, with sweet, pure water to wash down the food from their gardens. Having drunk snowmelt from the very mountain peaks, it seemed as if they themselves were brothers and sisters of the Five Holy Mountains.

Above them hung the glitter of the stars, below the glisten of snow-flakes and lapping water. And in the lake floated the reflection of Moon and the yellow Dog Star.

Coyote sat back on his haunches and howled his music at the sky.

# About the Stories

All these stories have been passed down from generation to
generation by word of mouth and changed a little by each successive story-
teller, growing and altering to suit the listener. I have retold them - sometimes
from the briefest passing reference in dusty old volumes -
to please you, the reader.
In doing so, I have made sometimes small, sometimes large changes, but have
tried to preserve an inkling of the pleasure each story gave to its original audience.

*G McC.*

### Juno's Roman Geese    *66*

Geese were sacred to the Roman goddess Juno, for they were said to share her attributes of love, guardianship and good housekeeping. Camillus (and perhaps the temple geese) is said to have saved Rome from Gaulish invaders in 365 BC.

### John Barleycorn    *74*

Wherever barley is grown, the agricultural cycle of sowing, growing, ripening, reaping, threshing and brewing has been celebrated in song. The subject of the song? John Barleycorn himself, indestructible spirit of the crop.

### The Singer Above the River    *77*

On the banks of the River Rhine, just south of Koblenz in Germany, a rocky bluff disturbs the flow of the river, creating dangerous currents and dismal rumours of evil magic . . .

### How Music was Fetched Out of Heaven    *84*

A sixteenth-century Nahua poem written in Nahuatt, language of the Aztecs, revealed this myth dating from a thousand years earlier. Quetzalcoatl, the feathered serpent, appears in Mesoamerican myth in all manner of guises, from the wind to the planet Venus.

### Whose Footprints?    *89*

*Eshu turns right into wrong, wrong into right.* So runs the Yoruba song. The Fon people of Benin call him Legba, that mischievous assistant of God, who causes chaos and strife wherever he goes.

### The Death of El Cid    *94*

By 1080, most of Spain was occupied by Moorish Africans. Rodrigo Díaz de Vivar entered Moorish Spain and made conquest after conquest. In doing so, he achieved fabulous wealth, glory and a place in Spanish history, his life and character hugely romanticized into an heroic ideal.

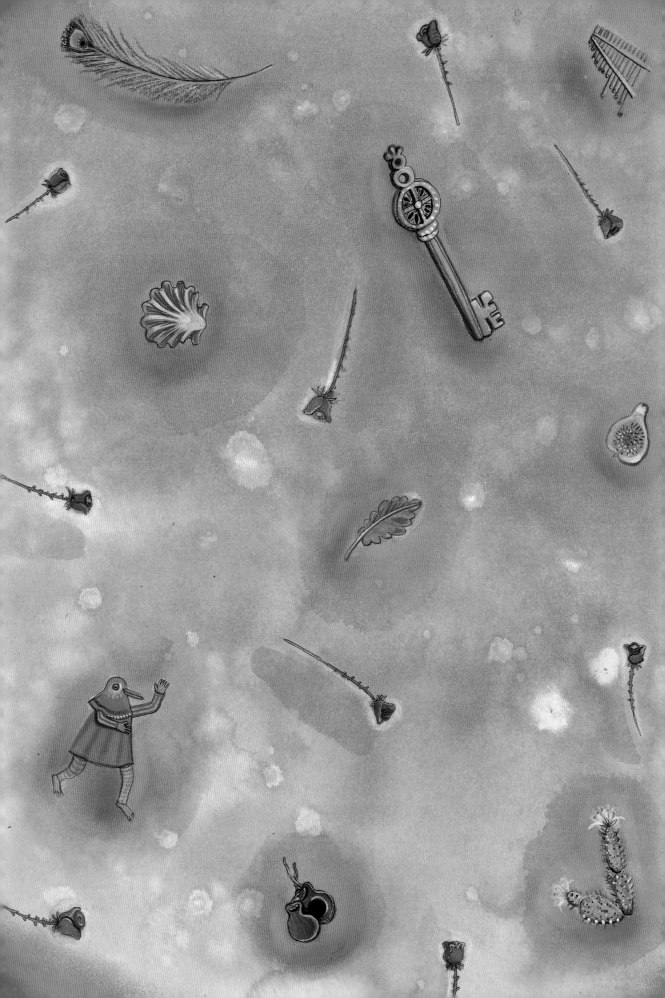